From the Foreword by Ervin Laszlo:

[This is] a book of insight as well as of foresight. A book important as few others. It provides essential orientation in our times of change — of accelerating critical change.

Praise for earlier editions

"A scientific romp and a spiritual adventure by one of the most adventuresome, exciting, and inspiring thinkers of our time. I hope it is widely read."

— LARRY DOSSEY, MD., author of *Reinventing Medicine*

"This book is written with impeccable logic and sound evidence drawn from a detailed knowledge of the worlds of physics, psychology, religion, evolution, and metaphysics. It is one of the most comprehensive books I have ever read, and makes the urgent point that it is time for humanity to flower into spiritual adulthood—or crash in its adolescence."

— *Body, Mind, Spirit*

"Here is a fascinating and involving picture of humanity's place in the universe and a bold portrayal of our possible destiny based on currently acceptable theories and ideas. This book is recommended to all living beings who plan on living in the future."

— *Whole Life Times*

"An extraordinary look at the inner spiritual crisis that lies at the root of the global challenges that face us as a society and a species. It takes a book of this magnitude to guide us toward those basic questions of who we are and where we are going."

— CHARLES GARFIELD, author of *Peak Performers*

"A wake-up call. Peter Russell calls upon his specialized knowledge in physics and spiritual disciplines, as well as a keen political sense, to bring us face to face with the present moment."

— MARILYN FERGUSON, author of *The Aquarian Conspiracy*

Waking Up in Time

PETER RUSSELL

Waking Up
in Time

Finding **Inner Peace**
in Times of **Accelerating Change**

Origin Press

Origin Press
PO Box 151117 • San Rafael, CA 94915
888.267.4446 • originpress.com

Origin Press is a division of Wisdom Media LLC
wisdommedia.us

Cover design by Phillip Dizick — pdizick@earthlink.net
(Based on the original cover design for the 1998 edition by Blue Design)

An earlier version of this book was published in 1992 by Harper SanFrancisco as *The White Hole in Time*.

Book design by Claudia Smelser Design, Berkeley
Special thanks to Joseph Sohm for the use of his photographs.
Photographic credits appear on p. 201.

Publisher's Cataloging-in-Publication
(Provided by Quality Books, Inc.)

Russell, Peter, 1946-
    Waking up in time : finding inner peace in times of accelerating change / Peter Russell. – Updated new release.
        p. cm.
    Includes bibliographical references and index.
    LCCN 2008929080
    ISBN-13: 978-1-57983-020-5
    ISBN-10: 1-57983-020-X

    1. Life. 2. Evolution. 3. Metaphysics.   I. Title.

BD431.R77 2008   110
                        QBI08-600155

PRINTED IN THE UNITED STATES OF AMERICA

10 9 8 7 6 5 4 3 2 1

Contents

The Quickening

The Crisis

Acknowledgments

Many thanks go to many people; without any one of them, this book would not be what it is. Anne Pauli lived through the whole of the book's gestation and birth, contributing feedback and criticism on just about every page. Ian Farquhar, Marilyn Ferguson, Oliver Markeley, Paul Wheeler, Judith Meynell, Lindsay Cooke, Cynthia Alves, Ruth Strasberg, Ray Gottlieb, Roger Evans, Bryn Jones, Leah Landau, Jane Henry, Chris Hall, David Wynne, Tessa Strickland, Juliet Weston-Lewis, Sheila Cane, Hag, Chris Coverdale, James Fraser, Edward Posey, Kindred Gottlieb, Joe Sohm, Jan Bakelin, Gisela Pauli, Roger Doudna, Robert Taylor, Christopher Bowers, and Sheila McCleod also read the book at various stages of its evolution and helped me clarify my thinking and expression. I'd also like to thank Marion Russell, Alexander Shulgun, Sylvia Timbers, Wendy Feldman, Pat Markeley, Terence McKenna, Linda Hope, Bill Whitson, Rupert Sheldrake, John Reilly, Willis Harman, Michael Toms, Mark Salzwedel, Eileen Campbell, and Anne McDermid, each of whom was of invaluable assistance in his or her own particular way. Julie Donovan was essential in the design and production of the 1998 version of *Waking Up in Time*. And last, but not least, my thanks also to my publisher Byron Belitsos and his book designer Phillip Dizick, without whom this 2008 release might never have appeared.

I would also like to thank Oxford University Press for permission to use the lines from Christopher Fry's play *A Sleep of Prisoners* and Harper & Row for permission to quote, from Stephen Mitchell's book *The Enlightened Heart*, his translation of the Rilke poem.

The Second Coming

Turning and turning in the widening gyre
The falcon cannot hear the falconer;
Things fall apart; the centre cannot hold;
Mere anarchy is loosed upon the world,
The blood-dimmed tide is loosed, and everywhere
The ceremony of innocence is drowned;
The best lack all conviction, while the worst
Are full of passionate intensity.

Surely some revelation is at hand;
Surely the Second Coming is at hand.
The Second Coming! Hardly are those words out
When a vast image out of Spiritus Mundi
Troubles my sight: somewhere in sands of the desert
A shape with lion body and the head of a man,
A gaze blank and pitiless as the sun,
Is moving its slow thighs, while all about it
Reel shadows of the indignant desert birds.
The darkness drops again; but now I know
That twenty centuries of stony sleep
Were vexed to nightmare by a rocking cradle,
And what rough beast, its hour come round at last,
Slouches towards Bethlehem to be born?

—W. B. Yeats

Foreword

In his preface to the third edition of this remarkable book, Peter Russell writes that he decided not to do a "complete overhaul" of its content to bring it into the twenty-first century because he considers that the essential thesis holds true today as it did fifteen years ago, when it was first committed to paper. He is entirely right: This book doesn't need to be updated, since it is not dated. It's a book of insight as well as of foresight. A book important as few others. It provides essential orientation in our times of change—of accelerating critical change.

Let me add a few thoughts of my own on the topic of accelerating critical change. Evidently, if change is both accelerating and critical, waking up "in time" becomes ever more important. Why we need to wake up, the author discusses with a clarity and insight matched by few others. How we need to wake up, he does likewise. But what can we say about the element of time—the timeliness of waking up? Russell emphasizes the great urgency in his new preface and this deserves to be taken seriously. It merits some further remarks to bring it fully into focus.

It is true that change is constant, and is constantly accelerating. But here constancy refers to the overall envelope of change—which goes on relentlessly—not to the rhythm and modality of change. Change is not even; in the language of science, it is not "linear." As Russell notes, it involves points of crisis which are at the same time points of opportunity—the opportunity to innovate. Crisis is the womb of creativity. But evolution, which is ongoing, progressive change over time, does not come with a built-in guarantee of success. Crisis can trigger creativity and produce innovation, but it can also produce breakdown. The biological record is littered with species that became extinct, and the history of humanity is littered with communities, cultures, and entire civilizations that broke down and disappeared. Modern civilization could go down in a holocaust; the human species itself could become extinct; and none of this would be exceptional in the annals of history and the records of evolution.

Wherever it occurs, progressive change follows a recognizable rhythm and modality. A basic beat holds true whether we look at the evolution of species or the development of societies; it in fact holds true for the evolution of all complex systems no matter what their particular origin, environment, and the nature of their principal components. These are systems that are both complex—made up of many different kinds of parts linked together through multiple networks on multiple levels—and open, receiving energy, matter and information from their surroundings, storing and using them, and then discarding, radiating, or communicating them back to their surroundings. These systems, as Nobel Laureate Ilya Prigogine has shown, are not in thermal and chemical equilibrium, that is, not in the inert "dead" state that is physically the most probable. Complex open systems are not even near such states; they exist in an entirely remarkable and intrinsically improbable far-from-equilibrium "third state." Stated another way, all living things and entire ecologies— even human communities—typically abide in this structurally unstable but dynamically self-stabilizing "third state."

This is important. We must know that the kind of stability that characterizes human beings and human societies is not the kind that characterizes a bridge, a building, or a dam. Expectations that the living world would be intrinsically stable are mistaken; there is a stability here, but it is not the stability of the Eiffel Tower, the Empire State Building, and the Aswan Dam. It is the stability of a human pyramid created by acrobats when they climb on each other's shoulders. This is not a structural, but a dynamic stability.

If wind, or an earthquake, shakes a well-constructed building, it moves, sways, dances with the pressure. Its structural stability has limits, however: a quake of catastrophic intensity can destroy even the best-conceived structure, as was seen in the partial collapse of the Bay Bridge in the 1989 San Francisco Earthquake. By contrast, the kind of stability that a human pyramid possesses is both more vulnerable and more resistant. It is based on a constant adjustment of all its elements to the strains and stresses that reach any one of them. If one of the acrobats loses concentration, he could fail to compensate for the small involuntary movements made by the others and the structure would collapse. In this proneness to collapse resides the structure's vulnerability. But the structure has an element of self-procured stability. When all goes well, every acrobat in the pyramid adjusts instantly to the changes that affect the equilibrium of the others.

Evidently, the higher the pyramid, the greater its vulnerability. But within the limits of the ability of the acrobats, it is dynamically stable. Unlike a building, a human pyramid is a self-adjusting, self-stabilizing system.

Complex open systems have the capacity to adjust to changes that affect their equilibrium. This is the reason why they can climb the ladder of complexity, notwithstanding the increased vulnerability that comes with their increased complexity. It is in this respect that today's world has reached the limits of its dynamic stability. This is not a surprise, and should not be a cause to despair. The beat of evolution is a sequence of states of dynamic stability interspersed with periods of critical instability. It is a constant, and constantly nonlinear, beat. The points of instability—also known as "chaos-points" or "bifurcation-points"—are not necessarily the preludes to disaster. They are tipping points; they lead either to the breakdown of the system, or to its breakthrough to a more sustainable form.

The constancy of evolution is the constancy of this basic beat, repeating over and over. It is also the constancy of the acceleration of the beat. As systems climb the ladder of complexity—inasmuch as they didn't fall off the ladder—the periods of dynamic stability become shorter, and the points of critical instability more frequent.

The evolutionary stability-instability dynamic, with its accelerating periods of stability and points of instability, comes to the fore in every process of progressive change. It is expressed in an exclamation known in some form in almost all cultures: "This is the last straw!" This saying refers of course (though we may have forgotten it) to the loading of weight on the back of a camel. Adding loads to the camel's back is a smooth, linear process: a little more load; a little more exertion by the camel to support it. But then comes the critical point: We add but a straw, and the camel collapses; we have reached the limits of its carrying capacity.

This "nonlinearity" recurs throughout nature. A living species can cope with changes in its environment—up to a point. When those changes accumulate, the stress reaches a critical point and the species dies out—unless, of course, it mutates. In relatively simple systems critical points lead to breakdown. In more complex systems these critical points can go one way or another. They are tipping points that do not lead inevitably to breakdown; they can lead to breakthrough.

This is well-tested theory, for these processes can even be simulated and mathematically described. This description of our current evolutionary challenge may seem like a merely abstract theory, yet it is far from abstract. At the present moment in history, it is the most concrete fact before us. It decides our future—even whether we have a future.

In human societies critical points create abrupt, and usually unforeseen change. In 1989 a group of East German refugees received permission to cross the iron curtain from Hungary to Austria. The penetration of a hitherto iron-clad barrier created that in-itself small but at the time critical shock to the Communist system that broke its back. It was "the last straw." In a matter of weeks the East European states seceded from the Soviet Union, and less than a year later the Soviet Union itself ceased to exist. The Soviet Communist Party, the most powerful political party in the world, not just lost power, it was outlawed. The republics that comprised the former Soviet Union did not disappear: after a period of chaos and near-breakdown, they managed to transform into the more open form in which they have maintained themselves ever since.

In the year 2008 it is not just one society or one system that is at the threshold of a critical tipping point, but the global community as a whole. The reason for this is unsustainability throughout the human world: economic, political, financial, social, and ecological unsustainability. Russell describes them in this book, and I have done so as well, in *The Chaos Point*. I need not rehearse them here. The point is that the outcome of these unsustainabilities is not yet decided. We still have what Russell calls a "white hole in time" and I a "chaos window." We can still reestablish dynamic equilibrium with each other and with nature.

In this book, Russell tells us what we need to do, and how to do it. We must wake up. Waking up starts with fostering inner growth—a timely and positive change in consciousness. This is a major challenge, but not an impossible one. Thinkers who have devoted their life to researching the evolution of human consciousness—Sri Aurobindo, Richard Bucke, Jean Gebser, Stanislav Grof, Don Beck, Ken Wilber, and Peter Russell himself—have forecast the coming of a more evolved consciousness, a consciousness that moves beyond the ego-bound insularity of the modern mentality to a deeper or higher "transpersonal" form. This could happen, and is even likely to happen. But we should add a word of caution. Though the outcome of the coming tipping is not decided yet, it will be decided before long—possibly (and I think very likely) by the end of the year 2012, the widely prophesied watershed in humanity's tenure on this planet. I say that because by that time many of the processes that drive our world to a critical point (and climate change is just one of them) will have become irreversible.

But the breakdown of our world is not fated. It will come about only if we refuse to change in the vain belief that tipping points either do not exist, or that they can be somehow managed once they appear. And there are feasible alternatives to going on as we have been: We could live, produce, and consume in a sustainable manner; we could relate to each other with understanding and mutual accommodation; and we could be respectful of the balances that define our world and accept to do our part to safeguard them. If we explore and make use of the alternative lifestyles, technologies, and relationships that are available to us, the tipping point known as 2012 will not be a prelude to disaster but the springboard to a sustainable world. This would not stop or contradict the evolutionary beat; it would make constructive use of it.

We must wake up in time. This, to my mind, means learning to act like the acrobats who maintain a human pyramid. If each acrobat were to think only of his own equilibrium, he would not respond in time to the pressures that affect the equilibrium of the others, and the entire structure would collapse. But collapse need not happen in the circus, and it need not happen in society. We can wake up to the many ties that bind us to each other and to our environment.

Sensitivity to each other has always been at the root of the kind of cooperation that enabled intrinsically unstable human societies to maintain themselves in their environment. In modern times we have suppressed this sense of connection to each other and to nature, but the connections themselves are there, and we can rediscover them.

The next evolution of our consciousness points in this very direction. It is the direction of transpersonal consciousness—a consciousness of unity with others and oneness with nature. This evolution will be vital for our future. It could reestablish the coherence we lack in today's world, a coherence found in well-integrated systems where all the parts are finely tuned to all the other parts. A human pyramid is just such a highly coherent system, and so is nature—and so is our body. But not contemporary society. We have filtered out the perceptions that would tune us to each other and to the environment; we've dismissed them as mere imagination or plain superstition. The result is growing alienation, fragmentation, frustration, violence, and chaos.

The next evolution of human consciousness could reestablish coherence in our world. If we allow it to unfold, the acceleration of the evolutionary beat will be matched by the growth of our ability to cope with the tipping points that come our way.

The future is open, and it is not bleak. There is no reason why humanity could not survive as long as humans with awakened consciousness walk the planet.

Ervin Laszlo
January 2008

Author's Preface to 2008 Edition

Much has changed since the second edition of this book was published in 1998—which is most fitting. The accelerating pace of life was one of the key themes of the book, and I was then predicting that humanity would experience as much change in the following ten years as we had in the previous twenty. This alone is not that new or breathtaking; many have commented on the increasing pace of change, and most of us experience its impact in on our lives. But the book went further, encouraging us to pause, to step out of our immediate concerns of home, family, job, finances, politics, and our next vacation, to consider where this accelerated change might be leading in the long term. I showed how, on the one hand, science and technology appear to be taking us ever-more rapidly into a world so radically different from today's that it may be quite literally "unimaginable." On the other hand, we are facing formidable challenges as ever-increasing material growth wreaks havoc upon the planetary systems that have nurtured and sustained us. The opportunities have never been greater; nor have the dangers been more severe.

The seeds of the book were sown fifteen years earlier. I had always been fascinated by accelerating rates of change—probably because the mathematician in me could see more clearly into the pattern and its long-term implications. I had already touched on this theme in my first book, *The TM Technique*, and developed it further in *The Global Brain*, so it was not unusual that one day I was talking with an acquaintance about this pattern in the history of economics. Then it dawned on me: This acceleration could not go on forever. Or even for very much longer. If civilization did not break down under the pressure of ever-more rapid change, then we were heading towards a point where the rate of change would become so fast it approached infinity. Mathematicians call this a singularity—a point where the equations run out, the laws break down, the patterns of the past no longer apply, and the future becomes undefined. I called this point a "white hole in time," and that became the title of the first edition of this book, published in 1992.

Today, the idea that we are approaching some kind of singularity is no longer so novel. In his best-selling books, *The Age of Spiritual Machines* (1999) and *The Singularity is Near* (2005), Ray Kurzweil has explored the implications of the exponential growth in the memory and speed of computer chips (often called Moore's law after Gordon Moore, the co-founder of Intel, who first drew attention to the trend in 1965). Kurzweil extrapolated Moore's Law to the time when computers would become smarter than humans. This, he projected, would happen around 2025. From then on, all bets were off. Our model of society breaks down when it tries to predict a future with smarter-than-human computers. We would have reached a singularity.

What Kurzweil and others are foreseeing is a technological singularity. But this would not spell the end of development, only a point in time when we would enter a radically different world. Change would continue accelerating, leading possibly to other technological singularities. But what about the overall pattern of ever-more-rapid change? Where is that leading? Our general development would seem to be spiraling towards a point of infinitely rapid change. This is the singularity that fascinated me—a singularity in the evolution of the human species.

A Crisis of Consciousness

However, the other side of the picture also has to be taken into account—something many proponents of a technological singularity fail to do. Our accelerating development has brought with it some very unwelcome side-effects. The human population has ballooned. More and more of us are consuming resources faster and faster. Half the rainforests have gone. Mineral resources such as copper, zinc, and nickel, are running out. We have extracted the easiest and cheapest oil; yet the world demand is still growing—a recipe for systemic meltdown. We are pouring waste into the oceans, atmosphere, and soil in ever-increasing amounts. The growing concentration of carbon dioxide in the atmosphere has begun affecting the climate, with untold consequences. We are in a global crisis—a crisis caused by the accelerated growth of humanity's ability to change the world for its own ends.

It is also a crisis in consciousness, a crisis in human thinking and human values. Take the case of climate change: Fifteen years ago, climate change was not on the collective radar. Today it makes newspaper headlines, shapes government policy, and is on almost everybody's lips. The problem lies not in a lack of technology. Renewable energy technologies—solar, wind, wave, and geothermal—have been around for decades. We could, if we put sufficient commitment to the task, develop and implement them to the stage where we could rapidly wean ourselves from our dependence on the fossil fuels of coal and oil. What holds us back is a lack of will.

For seven years, the Bush Administration in the US, then the largest producer of carbon dioxide, sought for its own political reasons to distort or deny the scientific evidence for global warming, and refused to sign the Kyoto protocol arguing that it would be bad for business (not recognizing, it seems, that if we do not meet this challenge there may be no business left to do). Meanwhile, China—which in 2007 overtook the US as the largest contributor of carbon dioxide—argued that it needed to develop its own economy, and continued opening two new coal-fired power stations per week. Nor were other nations really stepping up to the plate. The European Union struggled to get a commitment to reduce carbon emissions by 20 per cent by 2050, whereas most scientific research suggested we needed to reduce emissions by twice as much in half the time.

Of even greater concern is the growing awareness that if we do not act very quickly we may trigger runaway climate change, with catastrophic consequences. The most worrying scenario concerns the billions of tons of methane frozen in the permafrost of the Arctic tundra—a problem I singled out in the second edition of this book. As a greenhouse gas, methane is twenty-times more potent than carbon dioxide. The Arctic regions are warming three times faster than the rest of the planet, and are already two degrees warmer than they were in the 1980s. Consequently, large areas of the Siberian tundra are now beginning to thaw, releasing their methane into the atmosphere. This will lead to further rises in global temperatures, and even faster rises in the Arctic. The tundra will then thaw even faster, releasing even more methane. Within a short time, a global tipping point will be reached at which global warming becomes unstoppable. It will then only be a matter of time before the temperature rises the six or so degrees that would bring planetary catastrophe. Most of us are by now familiar with the projected consequences of a two-degree rise in global temperatures: more intense storms, longer periods of drought, crop failures in many developing countries, the destruction of nearly all the coral reefs, the melting of much of the polar ice, the flooding of many low-lying urban areas, the possible collapse of the Amazonian rain forest, and the extinction of numerous species.

If the temperature were to rise by six degrees, the prognosis is extremely bleak. At this temperature, the entire planet will be ice-free. Sea levels will rise by seventy meters. Many species of tiny plankton will cease to exist, and the problem would echo up the food chain, bringing the extinction of many fish and sea mammals, with similar repercussions for many species on land. Much more of the land would then be desert. Hurricanes of unimaginable ferocity would bring widespread ecological devastation. It would be a planetary catastrophe. If there were any human beings left, they would probably be reduced to small communities trying to eek out an existence in the polar regions.

Nor is climate change the only problem facing us. Our burgeoning material development has brought in its wake a number of other crises—food, water, resources, pollution—each with their own threats and challenges. Even if we do manage to curtail global warming sufficiently, these will each need dedicated attention if they are not to wreak their own brand of calamity. Moreover, they too need committed action now.

Unsustainable Consciousness

Twenty years ago, the phrase *sustainable development* was almost unknown. Today we are all familiar with the principle: It refers to development that meets the need of the present without compromising the ability of future generations to meet their own needs. Current practices are clearly unsustainable. We are raping the planet, leaving it hardly fit for our own needs, let alone future generations.

Behind our various unsustainable actions and behaviors lie unsustainable policies and practices. Behind them, human thinking and decisions, based on human needs and values. In the final analysis, it is our current mode of consciousness that is unsustainable. The real impediments to progress lie within our own minds. As the oft-quoted line from Einstein reminds us, "The significant problems we face cannot be solved at the same level of thinking we were at when we created them."

As well as doing everything we can to curb the tragic abuse of our environment and repair the damage that has already been done, we also need to do everything we can to step out of the materialist mind-sets that now prevent us from dedicating our full resources to the problems at hand. We need to move beyond our personal fears and prejudices; beyond the short-term, self-interested modes of consciousness that dominate too many of our thoughts and too much of our behavior. We need to wake up. Wake up to what we are doing, and where we are likely headed if we don't change. Wake up from the social trance that has us believing that, if only we could just get enough of the right things and experiences, we will finally be happy. We need to wake up to what is important, and what we really want. That was the call of the book—and it still is.

Re-valuing Spirituality

The world's various spiritual traditions have also called for such an awakening. In modern times, however, religion has had a bad rap. For a start, science would seem to have done away with God. Astronomers have looked out into deep space, to the far edges of the known universe; cosmologists have looked back into "deep time," to the beginning of creation; and physicists have looked down into the "deep structure" of matter, to the fundamental constituents of the cosmos. From quarks to quasars, they find no evidence of God. Nor do they find any need for God. The universe seems to work perfectly well without any divine assistance.

Yet the real concern of the spiritual traditions is not with the realms of deep space, time and matter, but with "deep mind," the one realm that science has chosen not to investigate. Those who have investigated this realm are the mystics, yogis, rishis, roshis, lamas, shamans, and other spiritual adepts who have explored consciousness first-hand—which, it could be argued, is the only way to explore consciousness. They have delved beneath the surface levels of the mind, observed the arising and passing of thought, and looked beyond, to the source of their experience and the essence of their own consciousness. There they have discovered how to free the mind from its material attachments, and through that find the ease and joy for which we all long.

Whereas Western science and technology has sought to relieve us from unnecessary physical suffering, the spiritual traditions have sought to understand how our minds become trapped in dysfunctional patterns and have developed various techniques and practices—we might call them spiritual technologies—that free us from the inner causes of suffering. They free us to act with more intelligence and compassion, so that we can attend to the needs of the situation at hand rather than the dictates of an anxious ego.

We need more than ever to re-evaluate spirituality. This does not mean a return to traditional religion; there is huge difference between spirituality and religion. Most of the world's spiritual traditions began with the awakening of an individual to what Aldous Huxley called the *Perennial Philosophy*—the wisdom that comes from an experience of unity with all things. This can be a profoundly transforming experience, so much so that many have sought to convey it to others. But their followers, being less enlightened than the teacher, tended to misunderstand some of it and forget other parts. What they did assimilate they passed on to others, who got even less of the original truth. Thereupon, the translation from one language to another and interpretation within existing belief systems, further distorted the original, and before long the religion that appeared was very different from the wisdom that inspired it.

Contemporary writers, such as Richard Dawkins, may be justified in criticizing religion for beliefs that fly in the face of modernity, and for the horrendous sufferings that adherents to one faith have inflicted on those of a different faith. We would, they claim, be much better off without religious belief. But to then dismiss spirituality altogether is to throw the baby out with the bathwater. Beneath the many surface differences in the world's spiritual traditions lies a common wisdom concerning how we become attached to our desires and aversions, and ways to liberate our minds from their dysfunctional egocentricity. This is one of our most critical needs, for, in the words of E.F Schumacher, author of *Small Is Beautiful*, "Our species is far too clever to survive without wisdom."

A Spiritual Renaissance

Whilst we are facing the gravest dangers to humanity, we are, I believe, also in the early stages of a worldwide spiritual renaissance. It began back in the sixties when many young people (and a few older ones) started exploring different modes of consciousness. It reached its symbolic zenith in the summer of 1967—the famous "summer of love"—with The Beatles' live recording of "All You Need Is Love," the first ever global satellite broadcast. This simple message has been at the core of all spiritual traditions. If we can love every other person and every other being, then the world would be many times better, if not ideal. But the question remains: How do we do that?

In the following years, people began looking to Eastern religions for ways to reach higher states of consciousness without using drugs. Training programs emerged purporting to encapsulate the essence of this wisdom. Books were written—so many that within twenty years the "mind-body-spirit" market had become the fastest-selling sector of the publishing industry. Today, we have unprecedented access to the spiritual teachings of just about every tradition and culture. We are discovering their common underlying truths, and translating that perennial philosophy into the language and terms of our own time. Something completely new is emerging: we are rediscovering that essential wisdom that inspired so many of the world's religions. But today we are discovering it together.

This search for awakening is following its own curve of acceleration. This pattern is to be found not just in terms of numbers of people involved, and the number of organizations, publications, and websites, but also in the quality of awakening. Forty years ago, our understanding and appreciation of spirituality was relatively naïve. Terms such as "cosmic consciousness" and "enlightenment" conjured ideas of being transported into a very different state, perhaps seeing the world bathed in light, or accessing some higher knowledge. While this may be possible, we have realized that such altered states of consciousness are not the essence of awakening. Rather than seeing a different world, it is more about seeing the same world, but in a different light. The quest for self-liberation is gravitating towards what is often called the "non-dual" position: There really is nothing other-worldly to attain, nowhere to get to. It is about being more fully present; it is about opening to the natural state of mind before it gets trammeled by attachments, aversions, and the machinations of the ego. From this perspective, there is nothing to do. Awakening is a letting go, an undoing of what keeps us apart from our true nature.

This, too, is not new. It has been a recurrent theme of many traditions; but today it has become the cutting edge of the quest for self-liberation. At the same time, a growing number of people are becoming fully awake, and proving themselves to be excellent teachers. Together, we are learning the most effective ways to awaken ourselves from our cultural trance. And the more we learn, the faster our awakening.

Collapsing Time

Can we wake up in time? Who can say? The future has always been hard to predict. And the faster change comes, the less reliable any prediction. When this book was first published, no one apart from a few computer scientists had ever heard of the Worldwide Web, let alone search engines, online shopping, and video streams. If we could not then predict just fifteen years ahead, we certainly cannot now. Nor, given the acceleration, can we foresee developments even ten years ahead. Perhaps the only thing we can say with certainty is that "the unexpected will out."

I wrote those words as the conclusion to an essay I was preparing on future scenarios back in 2001—on the evening of Sept 10, to be precise. Twelve hours later, I was awoken by a voice on my answering machine telling me the twin towers were down. The unexpected had arrived. A little sooner than expected.

For me, there was an added dimension to this momentous event. In previous editions of this book, I had sought to bring home how the rate of development had been speeding up, by charting the history of Earth up the side of New York's World Trade Center. On this scale, homo sapiens appears an inch from the top. The Greek and Roman empires thrived a hundredth of an inch from the top. And the whole of modern history occupies less than a thousandth of an inch—less than the thickness of the top layer of paint. What, I asked, did the next, even thinner layer hold in store?

When I was preparing the first edition of this book, I considered using an alternative parallel, imagining the history of life on Earth condensed into a year-long film, but finally decided in favor of the more visual image of what was then the world's tallest building. Today, six years after that pivotal day, this illustration has so many other associations it is no longer appropriate. So in this edition I have returned to my original idea. Modern history now occurs in the last frame of a year-long film. And the question becomes, what does the next frame hold in store?

Other than that, I have not made major changes to the book. Various facts and figures have been updated to bring the book more in line with current times, but the main text remains the same. I did consider a complete overhaul of the book in order to bring the content into the twenty-first century. However, as I started on that project, I realized it would effectively entail a whole new book. Yet I also saw that the essential thesis holds as true today as it did fifteen years ago. So I have left the book's main themes and structure as they were, letting them serve as a testimony to my thinking then, and to the times in which it was written.

Peter Russell
May 2008

To keep abreast of my current thinking on the issues discussed in the book, and other areas of my work, check my website The Spirit of Now at www.peterrussell.com.

The
Quickening

As once the wingèd energy of delight
carried you over childhood's dark abysses,
now beyond your own life build the great
arch of unimagined bridges.

Wonders happen if we can succeed
in passing through the harshest danger;
but only in a bright and purely granted
achievement can we realize the wonder.

To work with Things in the indescribable
relationship is not too hard for us;
the pattern grows more intricate and subtle,
and being swept along is not enough.

Take your practiced powers and stretch them out
until they span the chasm between two
contradictions . . . For the god
wants to know himself in you.

—Rainer Maria Rilke

Acceleration –
The Quickening Pace

T*he pace of life is speeding up.* Hardly the most startling statement. As most of us are only too aware, change comes more and more rapidly. Technological breakthroughs spread through society in years rather than centuries. Calculations that would have taken decades are now made in minutes. Communication that once required months occurs in seconds. Development in every area is happening faster and faster.

As a result, more of us are living in the fast lane—many in over-drive. We are faced with more information to absorb, more challenges

3

to meet, more skills to learn, and more tasks to accomplish. Yet the time to fit it all in seems to be getting less and less.

Worse still, there is no sign that things are slowing down. On the contrary, the pace of life is set to get faster and faster, taking us ever deeper into what Alvin Toffler called "Future Shock . . . the shattering stress and disorientation that we induce in individuals by subjecting them to too much change in too short a time."

Will we be able to cope? This, argued Toffler, is the challenge facing us: to learn to handle ever more rapid change without burning out or breaking down.

Not only is accelerating change putting us under stress; it is also putting increasing pressure on the planet. There are ever-growing numbers of us to feed, clothe, and house. Our waste is pouring into the air, the soil, and the seas many times faster than our environment can absorb it. Holes are appearing in the ozone layer, while forests are disappearing at alarming rates—as are the species that live in them. Seldom in its history has the earth changed so rapidly.

The faster the world around us changes, the more we are forced to let go of any cozy notions we might have about the future. No one today can predict with any degree of certainty how things will be in a year, or even in six months. When global stock markets can crash without warning, political walls crumble overnight, countries invade each other in a day, and ecological disasters shatter our illusions of control, we are increasingly forced to live in the present.

To live with continued acceleration and all the changes it brings will take more than simply learning to manage better. It will force a complete revision of our thinking about who we are, what we really want, and what life is all about.

An Eternal Trend

When we look back over history, it is clear that acceleration is not just a twentieth-century phenomenon. Change occurs much faster today than it did a thousand years ago; medieval architecture and agriculture, for instance, varied little over the period of a century. But even then change occurred much faster than it had in prehistoric times: Stone Age tools remained unchanged for thousands of years.

This increasing pace is not confined to humanity; it is a pattern that stretches back through the history of life on Earth. According to currently accepted theories—and it is well worth remembering that scientific theories change with time—*Homo sapiens* first appeared on Earth about a quarter-million years ago. Mammals started evolving much earlier, about 60 million years ago. The first living cells appeared much earlier still, some 3.5 billion years ago.

Nor did the trend begin there. Before any living system could evolve, other, equally important developments had to occur. This too was an evolutionary process that accelerated.

The Evolution of the Elements

Most cosmologists now believe that the Universe started somewhere between 8 and 15 billion years ago as an unimaginably hot and extremely compact region of pure energy. Intense internal pressures caused the Universe to expand very rapidly, creating the Big Bang. As the Universe expanded, it cooled and condensed into elementary particles: electrons, positrons, photons, and neutrinos. Cooling further, these particles began forming stable relationships with each other, giving birth to the very simplest of atoms: hydrogen and helium. Matter had been born.

It took millions of years, however, for more complex atoms to form. This could happen only when simpler atoms chanced to collide and combine. Over many eons, all the elements lighter than iron were created through this fusion process. But at iron, the chain stops.

The synthesis of heavier elements (e.g., cobalt, nickel, copper, gold, and uranium) requires the input of additional energy. This could not happen for several billion years, until the lighter elements had formed stars, and these stars had themselves become *supernovae*, the massive thermonuclear furnaces created when stars collapse in on themselves. From the supernova that preceded our own sun came most of the heavier elements we now find on planet Earth—and in every cell of our bodies. Matter had evolved, but it had taken ten billion years to create the hundred or so chemical elements.

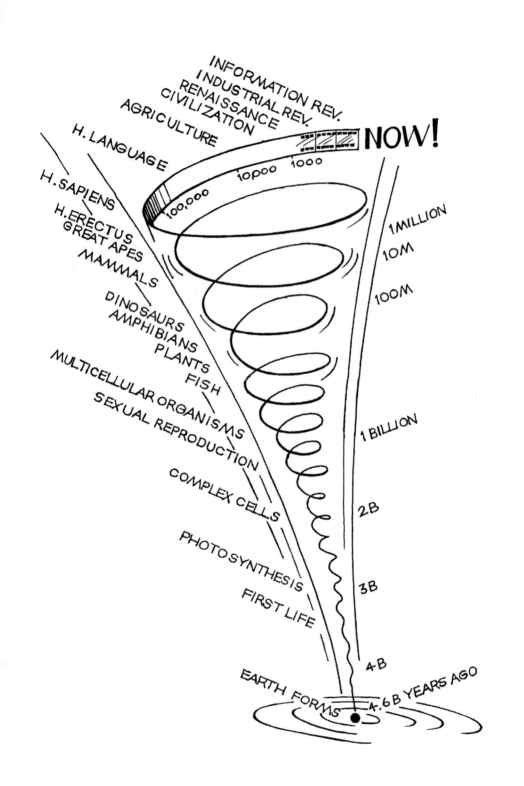

The Quickening of Life

This chemical diversity became the foundation stone for living systems, and as soon as life became established, the rate of development increased. Changes took place not over billions of years, but over millions — and, later, even faster.

Such lengthy timescales are so far from our everyday experience that it is hard to visualize just how rapidly evolution has been gaining speed. To get a better feel for these changes, imagine the evolution of life on Earth compressed into a film a year long — the ultimate epic.

The film opens on January 1st, with the formation of the sun and solar system. During the first month, the planet steadily cools and by early February the crust solidifies and the atmosphere and oceans form. In March the first simple living cells appear. In mid-May, the capacity for photosynthesis evolves, and with it the start of the plant kingdom. The oxygen these cells release accumulates in the atmosphere, promoting the appearance a month later of the first oxygen-breathing cells, and the beginnings of the animal kingdom.

More complex cells with a well-defined nucleus appear in mid-July, leading to the advent of sexual reproduction in late August, setting the stage for much faster evolution. In early September the first multi-cellular organisms appear, and over the next two months a rich diversity of life evolves in the sea. In mid-November fish appear. A week later the plants begin to colonize the land, followed after another week by the amphibians.

Dinosaurs rule the land for much of December, finally dying out just after Christmas.

Mammalian evolution takes off in the last week of the film.

Our early apelike ancestors make their debut on the last day, but not until seven o'clock in the evening do they walk upright. Homo sapiens itself arrives in the final fifteen minutes. It has taken 99.99 percent of life's journey to reach this step, and yet the story of humanity is just beginning.

Human language begins to develop five minutes before midnight. In the last minute of this year-long film, farming begins. The first civilizations, thirty seconds later. Buddha achieves enlightenment seventeen seconds before the end, and Christ is born three seconds later.

The Renaissance occurs four seconds from the end; the Industrial Revolution begins in the last two seconds, and World War II less than a half-a-second before midnight.

We are down to the last frames now, the last inch of 100,000 miles of film. The whole of modern history happens in a fraction of a second. The age of the microchip, rock 'n' roll, nuclear power, moon walks, global warming, and the Internet appear as the briefest flash.

One thing is clear: Wherever we are going, we are going there faster and faster.

But where are we going? What do the next frames in the epic film of life hold in store?

The Quickening of Spirit

If the pace of development continues to increase—and we shall see shortly that there is every reason to believe it will—then the amount of change that we have seen in the last twenty years will be compressed into the next ten years, or less, and after that into an even shorter time. This itself is not a new revelation; even so, it is not always fully taken into account in our extrapolations into the future. However, such constant acceleration has another, much more startling consequence—and one that is not usually considered at all.

We might imagine that this speeding up could continue a long way into the future; in a hundred years it would be much faster than it is now, and in a thousand years much faster still. But this sort of acceleration cannot continue forever. The timescales involved are getting shorter and shorter: from billions of years, to millions, to thousands, to centuries, and now to mere decades. If you plot out the curve of this sort of acceleration, you find that the curve soon approaches the vertical. In other words, the rate of change tends toward the infinitely rapid. Mathematicians call such a point a *singularity*; the equations break down and cease to have any useful meaning.

Whether or not humanity actually reaches this point of unimaginably rapid progress I shall leave for the moment. What *is* clear is that a trend that has been going on for billions of years is going to come to an end—and probably fairly soon. The general consensus of opinion among researchers in this area is that this singularity in time lies in the first half of the twenty-first century—assuming, that is, that we do not in the meantime turn the planet into a nuclear wasteland, accidentally create a plague that destroys us all, or change the climate to such an extent that the land becomes uninhabitable.

Some, such as Vernor Vinge, a mathematician at San Diego State University, see the singularity to be a consequence of technological acceleration, with ultra-intelligent computers creating an exponential runaway effect. But I believe technological progress to be but a phase in the overall pattern of development. Millions of years ago, it was biological evolution that was accelerating. Ten thousand years ago, the development of agriculture was speeding the rate of progress. A century ago, it was industrial breakthroughs. Today it is information technology that is pushing the rate of development ever faster. Tomorrow we may be in a new phase of progress. The exploration and development of human consciousness could take over from information technology as an even faster arena of quickening. If so, it would be spiritual evolution, not technological evolution, that takes us into the singularity.

To see how this might come about, and where it might lead, we must first go back and ask why it is that evolution tends to accelerate, and why, of all the creatures on this planet, human beings have created so much change so fast. We shall investigate why the exploration and development of the human mind is the next logical step in our evolutionary process, and why it is so critical for the world today. Our journey will lead us to consider what this inner development means on a personal level. How can it be encouraged and facilitated? And what might the future look like as we speed ever faster toward this singularity in time?

Feedback–
The Evolutionary Accelerator

The nature of the Universe loves nothing so much as to change things which are and to make new things like them. For everything that exists is in a manner the seed of that which will be.

—Marcus Aurelius

What do we mean when we say evolution has speeded up? The world of matter has not speeded up. As far as science can tell, electrons spin around the nucleus of an atom at the same rate as they did ten billion years ago. Nor have the biological processes that underlie evolution changed; they are probably still occurring at about the same rate as they did when life first emerged on Earth.

What has accelerated is the rate at which change has occurred: the rate at which new species have come into being, and the rate at which those species have evolved new characteristics. To borrow a term from the philosopher Alfred North Whitehead, what has accelerated is the rate at which novelty enters the world. The word *novelty* is used here not in its everyday sense of some unusual or curious circumstance, but in its literal sense of "newness."

Why has the rate of appearance of novelty accelerated? The answer is fairly straightforward, and has to do with what systems theorists call "positive feedback." It occurs whenever the current state of affairs promotes future growth. An example of positive feedback with which we are all familiar is the growth of population. The more people there are, the more children are born. The more children that are born, the more parents there will be in the future, and the more children will be born, and so on. If there are no constraints, the population keeps growing faster and faster.

Another common example in which the current state of affairs accelerates future growth is money invested at compound interest. A dollar invested at ten percent interest would be worth $1.10 after one year; $1.21 after two years; $2.59 after ten years; $117.39 after fifty years; $13,780.65 after a hundred years; and about $2,473,000,000, 000,000,000,000,000,000,000,000,000,000,000,000,000 after a thousand years, which is several trillion times the weight of the earth in gold. (Try collecting your interest on that!)

The growth curve of evolution is not as smooth or as mathematically precise as the growth of compound interest—the current view is that it progresses through a series of dramatic fits and starts—but positive feedback has nevertheless been at work at every stage.

A Platform for Life

The first molecules were simple compounds, composed of just a few atoms. As physical evolution progressed, these collected together into larger, more complex compounds. The more compounds that were created, the greater the possibilities for further combinations—and the more rapidly new molecules appeared.

Through this process, there emerged the highly complex macromolecules of RNA and DNA, which contain millions of atoms.

These brought with them a new and most significant characteristic: they could produce copies of themselves. Nature no longer had to build these macro-molecules through the combination of smaller subunits; instead, each molecule served as a template from which copies of itself could be built. And these copies served as templates for further copies. Nature had invented its own way of learning.

"Remembering" modifications from previous generations, living cells were able to "learn" those characteristics that enhanced their chances of survival. And the better they survived, the faster their numbers grew. In just one billion years of biological evolution, a far greater degree of novelty emerged on this planet than had appeared over the previous ten billion years of stellar evolution.

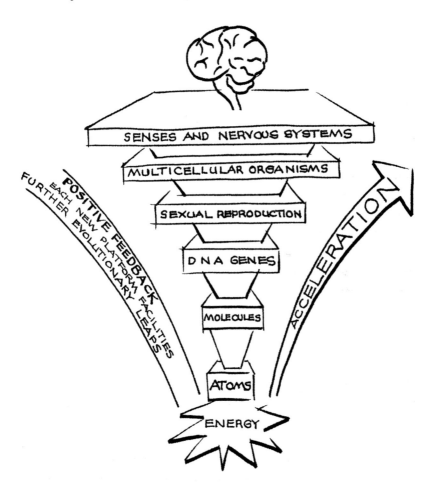

The Leap of Sex

Many of the new characteristics that evolved served as platforms for further developments. A good example is the advent of sexual reproduction, some 1.5 billion years ago. Until that time, cells reproduced by simply splitting into two, each of the new "sisters" being an exact clone of the original. The opportunities for beneficial variation were very small, and any that did occur were restricted to the descendants of that particular cell.

With sexual reproduction, however, two cells came together, shared their inherited genetic information, and produced offspring that possessed a combination of their genes. No longer did it take thousands of generations for just one genetic difference to arise. Differences now occurred in every generation, speeding the rate of arrival of novelty a thousandfold.

Cellular Cooperation

Multicellular organisms, the first of which appeared some 1,400 million years ago, were another great leap forward. Once cells were working together in a community, it became more efficient for individual cells to take on special functions. Some handled tasks such as digestion; some formed a protective skin; others helped the organism move about.

From then on, evolution was not limited to the creation of new species of cells. The muscle cells in a fish are not very different from the muscle cells in you or me. What has evolved is the way the cells are organized. This can change more easily and more quickly than the biological structure of the cells themselves. The result was another speeding up of development. The awe-inspiring diversity of species that we see on Earth today evolved in just the last tenth of Earth's history.

From Senses to Brains

As time went on, organs appeared that, in addition to processing energy and matter, could also process information. Some developed into senses capable of detecting changes in the environment; others became rudimentary nervous systems, able to convey information from one part of the organism to another and store it for later use. The well-being and survival of these creatures now depended not only on the genetic learning of their ancestors, but also on the learning accumulated during their own lifetimes. And again the rate of change accelerated.

Nervous systems are delicate structures, and the earliest ones, distributed throughout the organism, were very vulnerable. With the evolution of a spinal cord and skull, however, the nervous system was protected inside a case of bone. Once this step had been accomplished, the development of the nervous system itself became the major focus of evolution.

We tend to see vertebrate evolution in terms of the more visible changes in outer form—gills evolving into lungs, fins developing into arms and legs—but the most significant changes were taking place on the inside. The nervous systems of early worms occupied less than one ten-thousandth of the organism. The brain-to-body ratio of stenonychosaurus, one of the most intelligent dinosaurs, was probably about twenty times greater, but still not that impressive. With the advent of mammals, however, the nervous system began to grow very rapidly. Within the last fifty million years—less than one-third of the dinosaurs' total reign, and only a hundredth of Earth's history—brain size has exploded. In human beings, the brain now takes up one-twentieth of the body's weight.

As important as the increase in the relative size of the brain is the increase in its complexity. As the brain evolved, its structures became increasingly intricate. The cortex, the outer layer of nerve cells believed to be the seat of thinking and of higher mental functions, became much thicker and unfathomably complex. The brains of humans (and of whales and dolphins) are, with no exaggeration, the most complex structures in the known Universe—many times more complex than the largest computers such brains have yet designed.

This explosive development of the brain, occurring in just a few hundred thousand years, is one of the most dramatic and rapid changes in the whole of biological evolution. And on it rests the whole future of evolution. For through the human brain have come new creative potentials, new arenas for growth and development, and another leap in the speed of evolution.

Language –
The Dawn of Thought

Man is nothing but evolution become conscious of itself.

—Julian Huxley

To the casual observer, the most noticeable difference between human beings and the great apes is not our larger brains, but the uses to which we put them. Unlike chimpanzees or gorillas, and unlike any other creature on Earth, human beings wear clothes, grow food, paint pictures, sing songs, dig wells, mine coal, read books, go to school, get married, remember anniversaries, earn money, go to discotheques, hoard gold, hold elections, employ lawyers, belong to unions, take vacations, follow fashion, join fan clubs, collect stamps, give parties, fly planes, build highways, spray insecticides, stockpile nuclear weapons, and worship God.

17

Such differences stem from human beings' ability to think, to reason, to be aware of ourselves, to make choices, and to purposefully modify the world around us. Each of these abilities depends in turn on our exceptional capacity for language. Having brains several times larger than we need for our bodily functions gave us the added capacity necessary for the extremely complex neural processing involved in verbal communication.

Before this potential could be turned into speech, however, we needed a voice. Simply being able to make sounds is not enough; most animals do that very well. Nor is the possession of a larynx, or "voice box," sufficient; the great apes have well-developed larynxes. What makes the human larynx different are some important changes that it undergoes early in life.

At birth, the human larynx, like that of the apes, is high in the throat. In a child's first year, its speech is restricted and the sounds it makes are reminiscent of those made by young chimpanzees. But during the second year, the larynx moves to a lower position, carrying the base of the tongue with it. This change allows the tongue much greater freedom, so the child can begin to articulate a wide range of complex sounds. Speech becomes possible.

From an evolutionary perspective, speech represents a major step forward in information processing, as significant as the emergence of DNA, the evolution of sex, or the development of nervous systems. We can share our experiences, and hence our learning, with each other. Whereas a dog or cat learns primarily from its own experience of life, human beings learn not only from their own experience, but also from that of others—from those around us and from those who have gone before. Unlike other creatures, we do not have to build up our knowledge of the world from scratch; we can pool our experience and build a body of collective knowledge about the world.

Accelerated Learning

Estimating the rate of growth in our collective knowledge is a difficult task. One inspired attempt has been that of the French economist Georges Anderla for the Organization for Economic Cooperation and Development.[1] He takes the known scientific facts

---

[1] Quoted in *Prometheus Rising* and elsewhere by Robert Anton Wilson, a writer well worth reading.

of the year A.D. 1 to represent one unit of collective human knowledge. Assuming that our collective learning began with the appearance of language, it had required approximately fifty thousand years for humanity to accrue that first unit.

According to Anderla's estimates, humanity had doubled its knowledge by A.D. 1500. By 1750, total knowledge had doubled again; by 1900, it had become eight units. The next doubling took only fifty years, and the one after that only ten years, so that by 1960 humanity had gathered 32 units of knowledge. It then doubled again in the next seven years, and again in the following six years, taking us to 128 units in 1973, the year of Anderla's study.

Since then, it has continued to increase ever more rapidly. Today, with the advent of the information revolution, human knowledge is estimated to be doubling every eighteen months.

Whether or not one agrees with the details of Anderla's figures, the trend they reflect is clear. As soon as our species gained the ability to pool its individual learning, our development moved ahead at an unprecedented rate.

A Thirst for Knowledge

The advent of speech not only facilitated our communication with each other; it also gave us the ability to think in words, form concepts, and entertain ideas. We could begin to think about our experiences and understand them. As we did, we discovered order in the world around us. Not only did we see the stars; we observed the patterns in their movements. We could begin to draw conclusions and make predictions about the physical world. Science had been born.

We became a species with a thirst for knowledge, a hunger to understand. Why does night fall? Where does rain come from? What makes the wind blow? Why do rivers flow? Why do plants grow?

The answer to each question took us to a more intimate understanding of the Universe; and each answer left us with further questions. From where have we come? Why do we exist? Is there a meaning to life? Does creation have a purpose?

Awakening to Time

Our capacity to think about our experience made us aware of time in a new way. We could think about events from the past, deliberate on them, and learn from them. We could think about future possibilities and where we might be headed. We could speculate about events that had not yet happened, judge whether or not they would be beneficial, consider alternatives and their consequences, and consciously decide on our actions—and hence our futures. A new freedom of choice had been born.

We also became aware that our own time had a beginning and an end. We were faced with the inevitability of our death. We wanted to know whether or not we continued after our bodies met their end. Is there an afterlife? Or is this all there is?

Self-Reflective Consciousness

Being able to step back and reflect upon our experience gave humanity another distinctive ability. We became conscious of our own consciousness.

Consciousness itself was not new. Any creature that experiences its surroundings is conscious. A dog, for example, is aware of the world around it. It seems to feel pain, to recognize people and places; at night it seems to dream, perhaps chasing some imaginary cat. There is every reason to believe that what applies to dogs applies to other mammals—cats, horses, dolphins, rats—probably to all vertebrates—birds, reptiles, amphibians, fish—and perhaps to all creatures with a well-developed nervous system. But human beings are, as far as we know (we have not yet broken the communication barrier with dolphins and whales), the only creatures who are conscious that they are conscious. We can observe our thoughts and reflect upon our inner processes. We know that we know. We have a sense of self.

This has opened us up to what may be the most profound questions of all: "Who am I?" "What is consciousness?"

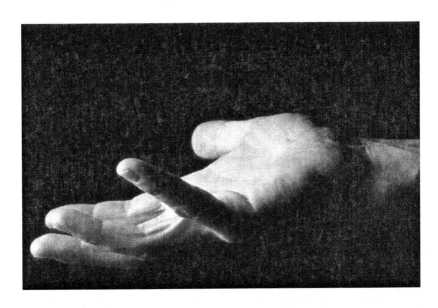

Hands –
Levers for the Mind

All tools and engines on earth are only extensions of man's limbs and senses.

— Ralph Waldo Emerson

H*omo sapiens'* capacity for speech and conceptual thinking may have enabled us to learn from each other's experience, to study the Universe, to plan our futures, and to become aware of our own existence, but these developments alone do not account for the many changes in our way of living that so distinguish us from all other animals. There is another feature of the human being that is essential to our prolific creativity: the human thumb.

Chimpanzees, gorillas, and several other creatures have thumbs, but only the human thumb can rotate completely about its base, and is fully opposable, meaning that it can touch, and be put in direct opposition to, each finger. This unique feature allows us to grasp objects of varying shapes and sizes, manipulate them, and perform delicate operations. It transforms the human hand into one of the most elegant and versatile biological organs ever evolved.

Combine this beautiful evolutionary development with an ability to reason and make choices, and you have a creature that can mold the clay of Mother Earth into a variety of tools.

Tools themselves are not new in the natural world: apes, for example, will use stones as hammers, and so will some birds. Human beings, however, endowed both with remarkable hands and with flourishing minds, became the most proficient and prolific tool users on the planet. We moved from pots and hammers to boats, plows, wheels, mills, drills, engines, planes, computers, and robots.

Through our hands, our ideas could manifest and take shape. We could invent new forms and could change the world in ways no other creature could. This newly found power to create tools constituted the second important platform on which human cultural evolution was built. From it came all manner of inventions and an explosion of novelty unprecedented in the history of life on Earth.

Amplification of the Thumb

One of our earliest inventions was agriculture. We began to irrigate the land, plant seeds, and store the harvest. Guaranteed a more reliable source of food, we were that much freer from the caprices of nature. We could ensure against floods or droughts, settle in one place, and build permanent shelters.

We discovered that through selective breeding we could create new varieties of plants and animals. This enabled us to accelerate evolution, and to direct its course. In just a few thousand years, we produced hundreds of different cereals from just a few simple grasses, and a thousand different breeds of dog, plus many varieties of fruits, vegetables, horses, cattle, and sheep.

At about the same time, we made another important discovery: the making of fire. All life's energy comes from the fire of the sun. Plants capture this energy through photosynthesis and pass it on up the food chain to animals. This is how we get the energy we require to walk, talk, and plant the crops that catch the sunlight. By burning wood, we created another means of liberating the energy stored up by plants. We could warm ourselves when the sun was down; we could survive cooler winters; we could move into new territories. Cooking food expanded our diets. Smelting metals allowed us to make more sturdy tools.

Several thousand years later came the wheel, creating both a revolution in transport and a wealth of new technology. The potter's wheel, the waterwheel, the windmill, the spinning wheel, the pulley, and almost every piece of machinery humanity has ever invented are dependent on the properties of the wheel.

The Industrial Revolution integrated the efficiency of the wheel with the energy of fire. Steam power replaced animal power and led to factories and increased production. Rail transport speeded communication and made resources and products more easily available. Steel led to revolutions in engineering. Pumps facilitated the mining of coal and minerals. And the mechanization of farming relieved many of the need to work on the land.

Here again, positive feedback was at work. New discoveries led to new machinery and equipment, and these led to other discoveries. Efficient pumps paved the way for hydraulic power, giving us the ability to apply great pressure and move heavy loads. Precision engineering increased the reliability of scientific tools and instruments. As we came to understand more about the structure of matter, we gained the ability to create new materials with new properties: alloys, ceramics, plastics. These could be used to create even better machine components, more efficient manufacturing processes, and yet more new products.

Electricity brought energy directly to the doors of factories and households, providing an easy source of light and heat. It was the power for a whole new generation of motors: large motors that enhanced the performance of industry, and smaller ones that led to a wide range of labor-saving machinery, from drills, washing machines, and vacuum cleaners to food mixers and electric toothbrushes.

In the area of transport, steamships gathered resources from the four corners of the world; the internal combustion engine made personal transport an affordable commodity; the airplane compressed weeks of travel time into hours.

Everything was accelerating: travel, communication, energy consumption, production, social development. We were constantly creating more change with less human effort.

Moreover, the rate of innovation was itself accelerating. In the early days of civilization, major breakthroughs were few and far between. Buckminster Fuller, the architect and inventor of the geodesic dome, estimated that about five thousand years ago, a significant invention occurred every two hundred years or so. By A.D. 1, there was one every fifty years. By A.D. 1000, the time had shortened to thirty years, and during the Renaissance it dropped sharply to about three years. With the advent of the Industrial Revolution, a significant invention appeared every six months; a hundred years later, every three months. By the middle of the twentieth century, the time had shortened further: humanity was creating major breakthroughs at the rate of one per month.

Some of our innovations are truly awe-inspiring; others may justify concern and anxiety. Yet, magnificent or fearsome as it may be, all our technology is, in essence, the amplification of the potential inherent in the human hand—guided by the human mind.

Information –
The Currency of Culture

To get to know each other on a worldwide scale is the human race's most urgent need today.

—Arnold Toynbee

The most rapidly growing technologies today are information technologies. Though they are sometimes referred to as "new technology," technologies that assist us in the processing of information are far from new. In fact, they are some of our oldest technologies.

Our first information technology was writing. Limited to speech alone, ideas could not travel far without distortion or loss. Writing enabled us to make more permanent records of our experiences.

Initially, we recorded our ideas on slabs of stone, but these were difficult to transport. The development of the pen and of papyrus overcame this handicap. Our learnings could then be shared with others in distant lands.

Convenient as they were, manuscripts had to be copied by hand—a process that was both slow and subject to error. This drawback was overcome with the invention of the printing press, 550 years ago. Over the next half-century, eight million books were produced. The philosophies of the Greeks and Romans were distributed, the Bible became widely accessible, and through various "how-to" books the skills of many crafts were disseminated, paving the way to the Renaissance.

The development of the telegraph, in the early 1800s, made it possible for the written word to be sent across vast distances. This was followed fifty years later by the telephone, linking people through the spoken word. The time required to convey a message across the world had dropped from months to seconds.

Twenty-five years later, the "wireless" freed people from the need to be linked by cable in order to communicate. Information could be made available to multitudes simultaneously.

Then came the phonograph, television, tape recorder, and photocopier, each amplifying further our ability to circulate information.

Today, computers have brought another breakthrough in information processing. More data than any human brain could ever process could be scanned, analyzed, evaluated, selected, and distributed . . . in seconds.

This enhanced processing capacity has had a positive feedback on material technology. It enabled us to design and build larger and more complex items—bridges, aircraft, dams, buildings, tunnels, boats, space vehicles—and to guide and control the processes of production, leading to increased automation in almost every area of life.

The more our technology advanced, the more did our ability to gather and process information. Progress fed back on itself in an ever-tightening spiral, increasing the pace at every turn.

Ephemeralization

Not only are we doing more, we are doing it with less and less—a process that Buckminster Fuller called "ephemeralization." The dome of St. Peter's Basilica in Rome, the largest of its time, took 5,000 tons of stone and forty years to build. Today we can build a carbon-fiber geodesic dome of the same size weighing only a few tons, and erect it in less than a week.

Similar changes have occurred in communication. A quarter-ton satellite can relay more information between Europe and North America than 175,000 tons of copper cable, using a fraction of the energy. The latest optical fibers have the potential to carry 25 gigahertz of information per second, which is about the volume of information that flows over all the telephone lines in the U.S. during the peak moment on Mother's Day, or the capacity to transmit all twenty-five volumes of the *Encyclopaedia Britannica,* including the pictures, in three seconds—all that in one thread of glass as thick as a human hair.

As successive generations of computers moved from the switching of relays to the switching of vacuum tubes to the switching of transistors (and soon, possibly, to the switching of molecules, or even atoms), computers have very rapidly decreased in size, and equally rapidly increased in power. Today's laptops have more memory, more flexibility, more functions, and more versatility (and are far faster) than the computers of 1960, which typically required about 2,000 square feet of space just to house them.

The exponential increase in computer memory is reflected in Moore's Law, which states that memory capacity doubles every eighteen months. Computer speed follows a similar pattern. Ten years ago, a 10-megahertz chip was the norm; five years ago, the norm was 100 megahertz. Today 1,000-megahertz (1-gigahertz) chips are commonplace, allowing real-time speech recognition, simultaneous translation, and a host of other capabilities that were science fiction only a few years ago.

As the power-to-size ratio of computers has exploded, so have their numbers. When the first computers were built in the mid-1940s, Thomas Watson, the founder and chairman of the company International Business Machines, said, "I think there is a world market for maybe five computers," and decided the business was too small to be worth exploring. Twenty years later, the company had shortened its name to IBM, and become the largest computer company in the world. Today 300,000 computers are being manufactured *each day.*

And these are just the computers we see. Three to four times that number are produced to be embedded in cars, printers, television sets, and cameras, all of them geared to increasing our efficiency—and hence to pushing the pace of life ever faster.

Global Interconnection

The communications revolution has also furthered humanity's integration into a single learning system. The ability to exchange ideas and experiences instantaneously that began with the emergence of language is now possible worldwide. Artificial satellites, fiber optics, digital coding, computerized switching, faxes, video links, and other advances in telecommunications have woven an ever-thickening web of information flowing around the world: billions of messages shuttling back and forth at the speed of light. We, the billions of minds that make up this huge "global brain," are being linked together by the "fibers" of our telecommunications systems in much the same way as are the billions of cells in each of our brains.

Through this rapidly growing network of light, we can share ideas and experiences not just with those around us, but with anyone, anywhere on the planet. We are moving beyond civilization, in its literal sense of "making into towns," into globalization. We are moving into a world without walls, where distance is no separation. Today I can call up a friend on another continent and have as close a conversation as I could with someone in the same room—so close, in fact, that I can easily forget that our bodies are separated by thousands of miles.

The most obvious example of this global integration is the Internet. Originally intended for military use, it was quickly adopted by scientists as a means of exchanging ideas and research. Then came the World Wide Web. When it was first launched, less than twenty years ago, it was intended only for text. Shortly afterward, it was decided to exploit its image capabilities, developing the graphical interface we know so well. Then came audio- and video-streaming, opening the door to video teleconferencing and even global broadcasting. Who knows where it will be in another two years? Indeed, the pace of change is now so fast that possibly no one knows. Right now there are probably thousands of software developers burning the midnight oil creating some new Internet tool. When it hits our screens in another six months or a year, it may trigger others to see novel applications that could radically change the way we think about and use the Internet. As ever, creativity breeds creativity, driving the spiral of development ever faster.

Creativity –
From Genes to Ideas

If I had to define life in a word, it would be Life is creation.

—Claude Bernard

Humanity's unprecedented powers of thought and action have established us as a most significant species on planet Earth. But our evolutionary significance does not end there. Our minds and hands have produced a new source of novelty, putting at nature's disposal a fundamentally new mechanism of evolution.

If we move to a cold climate, we no longer have to adapt by evolving a thicker coat of hair, more fat, or changes in metabolism—a process that, even with selective breeding, could take thousands of years. Instead, we can design and build insulated houses, central heating systems, and warmer clothing. If we choose to fly, we can study aerodynamics and build wings for ourselves; we do not need to go through the long slow process of biological evolution as birds and flying insects did. If we want to step into the vacuum of space, we can conceive and create ways to take essential life-support systems with us. And if we don't like our genetic constitution, we can re-engineer it.

A New Source of Novelty

Most people do not usually consider humanity's technological developments to be part of evolution. This is largely because twentieth-century scientific thinking considers evolution only in terms of the development of different biological species and the underlying genetic processes. Yet before Charles Darwin, the word "evolution" had a much wider general usage. Its original meaning is the "rolling out" of the world: the emergence of new forms and phenomena from existing ones. In those days, the term was applied to the world in general, including the world of ideas, not just to living creatures.

Prior to biological evolution there had been, as we saw in the first chapter, a process of physical evolution. New atomic elements were created from combinations of existing atoms; as these formed into compounds, new substances emerged, bringing new properties to matter. Only later, after the material universe had evolved into very large and complex molecules capable of self-reproduction, did genetic processes begin molding the clay into a rich variety of living forms. Now, with the appearance of *Homo sapiens*, a new form of evolution has become possible. It is our minds and hands that are doing the molding, reorganizing matter into new structures and creating new capacities.

The human mind has now become the dominant creative force on this planet. The whole panorama of change that humanity has initiated, the whole of the culture that differentiates us from every other creature on this planet, started as ideas in the mind.

Unnatural Creations?

Many think that humanity's creations are not natural in the same way as the results of biological evolution are. Why is this? We do not consider a beehive to be less natural than a bee, a beaver's dam less natural than a beaver, or a bird's nest less natural than a bird. Why should creations that come through the human mind and hand be any less natural?

Why do we think a lamppost is less natural than a tree? It is true that they were created in different ways. One is a product of biological processes, the other a design of the human mind. One is a living system and the other inanimate. We may judge one more beautiful than the other. But are they any different in the eyes of the Universe? Both are experiments in design. Both result from eons of evolution.

The different way we perceive many human artifacts stems from the effects they have on the world. When these effects do not seem to be in harmony with the rest of nature, we regard them as "unnatural." But the reason they do not harmonize with nature is that the thinking that governs their creation and use is not in harmony with the rest of nature. Believing we are masters of nature, rather than agents within it, we often use our unprecedented creative potential for our own ends, resulting in actions that do indeed separate us from the rest of nature. As a result, our creativity may frequently be misguided. But it is not unnatural.

A Giant Leap for Evolution

Evolution mediated by human minds and hands has been able to create in years developments that would have taken genetic processes alone millions of years—or that might never have occurred at all. The solar cell, for example, represents a totally new method of capturing the sun's energy—converting it directly into electricity. This is as significant a breakthrough as the development of photosynthesis itself, some three billion years ago.

Radar has allowed us to "see" in new ranges of frequencies—a development as significant as the evolution of the eye.

Through nuclear physics, we have discovered how to create new chemical elements. The last time such a synthesis occurred in our area of the Universe was in the supernova that preceded our sun, some five billion years ago.

Genetic engineering means that the creation of new organisms is no longer dependent on the slow process of biological evolution; we can consciously design and create them within a matter of months. (Whether we will use this awesome power wisely remains to be seen.)

And we have made our first journeys out into space and walked on the moon—a step that biological evolution alone might never have achieved, not in ten billion years.

In short, the shift from genes to ideas represents not just another step in biological evolution, but a giant leap for evolution itself. We, the products of this long evolutionary development, have now become conscious participants in the continuing unfolding of creation.

Today —
Foundation for Tomorrow

"A slow sort of country!" said the Queen. "Now, *here*, you see, it takes all the running you can do, to keep in the same place. If you want to get somewhere else, you must run at least twice as fast as that!"

— Lewis Carroll

All human progress has come about in what, from an evolutionary viewpoint, is virtually no time at all. We are the product of an ever-tightening spiral of development that has condensed timescales from billions of years to mere decades.

And there would seem to be no end to it. Advances in science, technology, communications, education, health care, and culture are all bound together in a multidimensional feedback loop. We are learning faster, growing faster, moving faster, and changing faster. In one year, we experience more innovations than the Pharaohs did in a century.

Looking to the future, one thing seems certain: whatever form development may take, its pace will continue to increase. New discoveries and new technologies will lead to further new abilities and new ways of changing the world. Creativity will continue to breed creativity.

Saving Time

As if these pressures for further change were not enough, another factor is fueling the increasing pace of life: our attitude toward time. Much of humanity has become obsessed with time, particularly in those cultures that have experienced the greatest leaps in material development. Believing that time can be "saved," we seek to pack more and more into the time available. We shop in supermarkets to save the time it would take to visit several stores—and we like quick checkout lines. We build highways around and through cities so that we can reduce the length of a journey by fifteen minutes, and thereby pack a few more things into our day. We spend fortunes digging tunnels that will save us another half-hour. We construct noisy and polluting supersonic aircraft (and plan even faster ones) so that a very small minority can save a bit more time. And we create ever-faster microchips for ever-faster computers, so that software loads more quickly, pages are rendered faster, data is analyzed more rapidly, and a tiny bit more time is saved.

Any development that can do something more quickly has an advantage in the marketplace. Seduced by the idea of temporal efficiency, we focus much of our creative talent on getting more done in less time. With the extra time we have "saved," we pack in some more tasks—and then require another time-saving tool to cope.

However giddy today's rate of development may seem, tomorrow's world will, barring calamity, be changing even faster.

Wherever Next?

But again, where are we going? Where will our burgeoning creativity take us next? What does the next spiral in the film of life hold in store?

In the short term, technology will extend in some fairly predictable directions: Computers will become even faster, smaller, and more friendly, invisibly pervading almost every area of life; and the telephone, television, and computer will be integrated into a single multipurpose tool—in fact, already are in the case of the iPhone and related technologies. Increasing miniaturization and nanotechnology will lead to the creation of robots the size of living cells, or smaller. Medical science will extend human life by another decade or two, while genetic reprogramming and stem-cell research will offer new treatments for otherwise incurable hereditary diseases, as well as new drugs, new foods, new insecticides, and so on.

Yet, at the same time as we push ahead toward greater technological brilliance, the dangers of misapplying our awesome powers are also becoming increasingly apparent. Planet Earth is suffering badly from the impact of our waste. Its mineral and biological resources have been plundered. Its delicately balanced climate is being disturbed—perhaps irreversibly. Moreover, as resources dwindle, the tensions between peoples increase, and threaten to explode at the slightest provocation.

But one thing is certain: the future will be full of surprises. Who in 1900 would have predicted the solar cell, genetic engineering, nuclear weapons, radar, microchips, the personal computer, satellite navigation, lasers, television, DVDs, cell phones, or many of the other breakthroughs that we accept so easily today? They were all beyond the thinking of the time. Most of them were still beyond our thinking half a century later. Even twenty years ago, no one foresaw the impact that personal computers would have on our lives. Even science fiction writers got it woefully wrong.

How, then, can we be expected to foretell the next twenty years accurately? Or even the next five or ten years? We are likely to see as much change compressed into them as we have seen in the last twenty years. Most of the breakthroughs that are to come remain, quite literally, inconceivable.

Inner Evolution

One area where we may see some of the most exciting developments is the exploration of human consciousness. We still know very little about how sensory perception leads to awareness and how ideas come into being. We have very little understanding about our feelings, or about the ways in which our attitudes affect our perception and behavior. And the inner self, that most intimate aspect of the conscious mind, remains as mysterious as ever. This is the next great frontier: not outer space, but inner space. Moreover, research and development in this area is more than just an option; it has now become an imperative. In the chapters that follow, we will see how the crises in which humanity now finds itself demand that we undergo a fundamental shift in consciousness.

Our power to change the world may have made prodigious leaps, but our internal development, the development of our attitudes and values, has progressed much more slowly. We seem to be as prone to greed, aggression, shortsightedness, and self-centeredness as we were 2,500 years ago, when the Greeks were extolling their ethical philosophies and the virtues of self-knowledge. Many good words have been spoken over the intervening years; but how many have been lived?

If we are to continue our evolutionary journey, it is imperative that we now make some equally prodigious leaps in our ability to transform our minds. We must wake up and develop the wisdom that will allow us to use our new powers for our own good and for the good of all. This is the challenge of our times.

The
Crisis

Toy-bewitched,

Made blind by lusts, disinherited of soul,

No common centre Man, no common sire

Knoweth! A sordid solitary thing

Mid countless brethren with a lonely heart

Through courts and cities the smooth savage roams,

Feeling himself, his own low self, the whole;

When he by sacred sympathy might make

The Whole one Self! Self that no alien knows,

Self, far diffused as fancy's wing can travel!

Self, spreading still! Oblivious of its own

Yet all of all possessing! This is Faith!

This is the Messiah's destined victory!

—S. T. Coleridge, *Religious Musings*

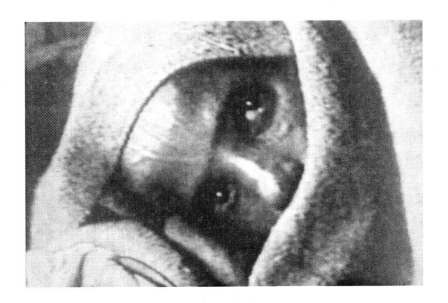

Crisis —

Sounding the Alarm

This we know—the earth does not belong to man, man belongs to the earth. All things are connected like the blood which unites one family. Whatever befalls the earth befalls the sons of the earth. Man did not weave the web of life; he is merely a strand in it. Whatever he does to the web, he does to himself.

—Chief Seattle

We may be living through the most stimulating and exciting times in history; but our rapid development has brought with it unexpected dangers, not the least of which is humanity's ever-growing size.

Ten thousand years ago, the human population numbered around ten million, gathered into small settlements. As the conditions of our lives improved, our numbers grew. By A.D. 1000, there were about 350 million of us. In 1650, the world population was about 550 million; by 1800, it was 900 million. Nineteenth-century advances in hygiene and medicine kept our numbers expanding, and by 1900 they had reached 1.6 billion. In 1950, there were 2.5 billion of us; by 1990, five billion; and in 1998, we passed the six billion mark. Luckily, there are now signs that this explosion is slowing. If current trends continue, the human population will probably stabilize somewhere between ten and twelve billion—a dauntingly large figure, but one that is sustainable, provided that we successfully tackle the various problems that follow in its wake.

Our rapidly growing numbers mean that there are more and more mouths to feed, more and more bodies to clothe, and more and more people to house. There are an ever-increasing number of tools to manufacture, and a growing amount of waste to dispose of, and much more energy is required to do it all. As if these problems were not difficult enough, our technological development is magnifying the demands made by each person. The average city dweller of today uses far more energy and resources than did a peasant farmer two hundred years ago. There are all those household appliances we use, plus the energy and resources it took to create them. We have central heating and air conditioning; we travel to work and for leisure; we ride the elevator and use many other labor-saving (but energy- and resource-consuming) conveniences. There is the growing and processing of the food we buy in the supermarket, its packaging and its transportation. And there is the share we all have in the material infrastructure of our society: government buildings, defense projects, emergency services, scientific research, and so on. Estimating our total energy and resource consumption is not easy, because of the many factors that must be taken into consideration, but all the estimates I know of suggest that each of us consumes somewhere between two hundred and one thousand times the energy and resources of a person living before the Industrial Revolution.

This added per-capita consumption, when compounded by our growing numbers, results in an even greater impact on the planet. There are now ten times as many people in the Western world as there were 300 years ago, and if we take only the more conservative estimate of a two-hundredfold increase in individual consumption, the combined effect for the whole of our society is a two-thousandfold increase in consumption. This means that in one year we now consume more energy and resources than we would previously have consumed in two thousand years. Or, to put it even more strikingly, we now consume more in one year than we did in the whole period from the birth of Christ to the dawn of the Industrial Revolution. Little wonder that we are in crisis.

The Price of Fire

Most of the energy we have used has been obtained from the taming of fire—initially from the burning of wood and dung, but later from coal, oil, and gas. Before the dawn of civilization, forests carpeted most of the land, and had wood been used only to keep us warm, the land might have stayed that way. However, our developing technologies were also hungry for wood: wood to fire the kilns that produced pottery and bricks, wood to build houses and boats, wood to construct carts, plows, and other machinery. The result was deforestation.

The faster humanity developed, the more rapidly the forests disappeared. In Europe trees were felled to provide both fuel and timber, and the cleared areas became fields (the word is derived from *felled*) to grow food for the swelling population. As the European forests dwindled, the forests of North America were plundered. The ships that brought the early settlers over from Europe went back laden with timber for the new railways and factories.

Today, less than 20 percent of the earth remains forested; yet our demand for wood is greater than it has ever been. The consequence, as we are all well aware, is the plundering of the largest remaining forests: the tropical rainforests of South America and Southeast Asia.

I remember the first time I flew across the Brazilian forests at night. I looked out the window and saw what looked like the thin red line you see along the edge of a smoldering piece of paper. The only problem was that the line was ten miles long, and it was not paper but forest that was burning. According to the World Wildlife Fund, more forests were burned around the world in 1997 than in any other year in recorded history. At least 12 million acres of forest and scrub—an area nearly the size of England—burned in Indonesia and Brazil, along with vast areas of Papua New Guinea, Colombia, Peru, Tanzania, Kenya, Rwanda, and the Congo. Jean-Paul Jeanrenaud, head of the fund's forest program and one of the report's authors, said, "1997 will be remembered as the year the world caught fire."

Climate change is also making forest fires more likely. In California, for example, climate change has brought a half-degree centigrade rise in average yearly temperature across this region, and the fire season in Southern Califonia is now on average 78 days longer than it was in the late 1980s. No one really knows what the long-term effects will be across the planet. The rainforests are an important organ of the biosphere and exert a considerable influence on the earth's climate. Moreover, the destroyed areas cannot easily be reclaimed. The soil that remains is relatively poor and, after a few years of grazing, collapses into desert.

As we destroy the forests, we also eradicate entire species of plants and animals. No one knows how many millions of species there are on Earth; scientists think that we have discovered only ten percent of the total. And no one knows how fast they are disappearing. Current estimates suggest that something like ten thousand species become extinct every year, that is, about one every hour. One thing we do know is that the survival of life on Earth depends on the rich diversity of species. How many more can be destroyed before the planet's biosystem collapses?

A Warmer World

The second price we have had to pay for fire has been a warming we did not intend: global warming.

The principal waste product of fire is carbon dioxide. This is not in itself a dangerous gas; indeed, it is crucial to the life of plants, and, given time, the biosphere could absorb all the carbon dioxide that we produce. The problem is that we are now producing this gas far faster than the oceans and plants can absorb it. As a result, the carbon dioxide content of the atmosphere has risen by about one-third over the last thirty years, with potentially serious consequences for the planet's climate.

The more carbon dioxide there is, the more heat is trapped by the "greenhouse effect," and the warmer the atmosphere becomes. The full impact of this warming is becoming increasingly certain: It has the potential to trigger changes that radically alter the course of life on Earth.

Most of us now know that global warming, at its current rate of increase, is likely to lead to a melting of the polar ice caps and a consequent rise in sea levels, leading to the flooding of lowland areas such as Bangladesh, the Netherlands, and many of the world's coastal cities, with all its ensuing problems and enormous costs. But there are other possible consequences of even greater concern. Vegetation would not be able to "migrate" as fast as the changes in climate occur; many temperate forests would vanish, adding further to climatic instability. Areas that we rely upon for much of our food, such as the grain prairies of the U.S., may suddenly become arid.

Shifts in climate could also lead to changes in ocean currents such as the Gulf Stream, which circulates heat from the tropics to Western Europe. If this were to occur, countries such as Britain could be in for a dramatic cooling rather than a warming. Hurricanes, which are seeded by warmer tropical waters, are even now increasing in both frequency and strength.

Even a modest global warming could trigger a runaway effect. Frozen in the tundras of northern Canada and Russia are vast amounts of methane, which is an even more potent greenhouse gas. If these areas thawed, releasing their methane into the atmosphere, the world would warm much faster. This is without the current doubling in methane produced by all the cows we keep, by the rice paddies that are growing in step with our population, by decomposing swamps, and by the termites that feed on the dead wood in our dying forests. Water vapor itself is a greenhouse gas; as the air becomes warmer and more moist, the heat trapped in the tropical regions will increase even further. Deforestation does not help, either; it reduces the biosphere's capacity to absorb carbon dioxide. Moreover, the warmer the world becomes, the faster dead vegetation will decay, both on land and in the sea, further speeding the release of greenhouse gases.

As a result of these and other feedback loops, the earth's temperature is now rising much more rapidly than we initially suspected. Summarizing this runaway scenario in the British science magazine New Scientist over a decade ago, John Gribbin has warned that if this happens, "the greenhouse threat facing us is worse than any forecaster has yet dared to imagine." This threat is now coming to pass.

Recipes for Disaster

Carbon dioxide is just one unwanted waste product of our industrialization. Automobiles, power stations, and chemical plants pour poisonous gases into the atmosphere, to fall later as acid rain. As the acidity of rivers, lakes, and soil rises, the fauna and flora suffer. In Central Europe, as many as half the trees have suffered or died, and the damage in Eastern Europe, where pollution has been more severe, has been even more disastrous. In Scandinavia, entire lakes are dead. And we are only just beginning to recognize the effects of acid rain on human beings.

Meanwhile, we dump our chemical garbage out of sight under the soil, only to find it later seeping into our water supplies. Or we pour it into the sea, killing not just fish but other organisms crucial to the ecological balance.

As if this were not enough, shortsighted intensive agricultural practices turn soil into sterile dust, to be washed or blown away. At the present rate of loss of twenty-six billion tons per year—that is, five tons per person per year—there will be no soil left in a hundred years.

Most dangerous of all, the ozone layer in the upper atmosphere, which protects life on land from the sun's damaging ultraviolet rays, is being destroyed by chlorofluorocarbon (CFC) gases. With CFCs, we have done more than release a pollutant; we have released a catalyst, a substance that speeds up other reactions without itself being changed. One CFC molecule can destroy tens of thousands of ozone molecules, and can continue doing so for many decades before it is itself destroyed.

Along with the new reports of thinning ozone, we are faced with pictures of children in Australia and New Zealand who have to cover their skin and wear broad-brimmed hats, and with estimates of the increases in skin cancers and eye cataracts that are likely to result from the increased exposure to ultraviolet light. But skin cancers and eye cataracts will probably be the least of our worries. What will happen to other creatures? We cannot fit bees with sunglasses, and blind bees will not be much good as plant pollinators. The consequences of that could be catastrophic. And what about the effect of increased UV light on plants? The most vulnerable parts of plants are the growing tips. Destroy the DNA in these cells and the plant will not reach maturity, and will not seed—with equally catastrophic consequences. Or consider the effects on the microscopic phytoplankton in the sea, which have no skin to protect them and are very vulnerable to ultraviolet radiation. Destroy these and the planet's food chain will crash.

If we do severely damage, or even destroy, the ozone layer, life on land will become nearly impossible. For half a billion years, the ozone layer has shielded the planet from ultraviolet light, making it possible for plants and animals to emerge from the sea and colonize the land. Without this protection, the only life that could survive would be beneath the surface of the sea. We would have destroyed half a billion years of evolution—and ourselves with it. That is how dangerous our situation is.

The severity of the threat posed by CFCs is so great that two major international agreements have been made in an effort to halt their production. In some respects this has been a major success story; it shows what can be achieved when the nations of the world put their minds to a critical task. But this does not mean the danger has passed. The CFCs released during the past two decades will continue to wreak their havoc for up to fifty years or more. Moreover, it is now being realized that the effects of global warming on the upper atmosphere could led to further reductions in ozone. If we are to survive we are going to need a similar degree of global commitment to the various other problems confronting us, and these are a going to involve much more radical personal, social, and economic changes than phasing out CFC production.

Other Threats

It need not be environmental disasters that claim us. As the peoples of the world become ever more intimately linked, we become increasingly vulnerable to plagues. Some years ago, scientists working for the U.S. government conducted a simple experiment. They sprayed harmless bacteria into the departure lounge of Washington's National Airport. Hitching rides on the passengers and transferring onto others at their destinations, the bacteria spread from person to person. Within three weeks, they were to be found in nearly every part of the U.S.

We should count ourselves lucky that AIDS is not spread as easily; we would all have been infected before the first case had been diagnosed. Who knows what other diseases are lurking, waiting for conditions that will make them epidemic, or what diseases we might inadvertently create through genetic engineering? Moreover, should a new plague appear, we would find that our overenthusiasm for antibiotics has left our bodies weakened and our medical armory poorer. With the passing of time, our vulnerability rises rather than falls. Several bacteria that were once treatable with drugs are developing resistance to every one of our antibiotics. At present, we are managing to contain such bugs in hospitals, but they could break out at any time.

Finally, we should not overlook the ecological effects of war. Military operations consume much of the world's oil production and many of the earth's resources. Nor is modern warfare good for the planet. Agent Orange, napalm, biological weapons, and high explosives have a far more devastating impact than bows and arrows or cannonballs.

So far, we have managed to avoid the horrors of a nuclear war, but it remains an ever-present danger. As resources become less plentiful, food and water become more scarce, the gap between rich and poor grows, and climatic change promotes mass migrations, it is not difficult to imagine a number of scenarios leading, either accidentally or deliberately, to a nuclear conflagration.

The Totally Unexpected

As likely as any of these scenarios are some that remain totally unexpected. The appearance of the first ozone hole over Antarctica was a surprise. Scientists had known for twenty years that CFCs would deplete the ozone layer, but none of their models had predicted an ozone hole, nor was the idea among their hunches. Indeed, so surprising was the data that the computers analyzing it systematically rejected it for several years.

Our knowledge of ecology and global climate still contains so many gaps and gray areas that other unanticipated changes are virtually certain. There may be unforeseen flips in the weather, unexpected changes in ecosystems, surprising responses by other species, or unpredicted earthquakes in significant locations. All we can say with certainty is that change will come—and more and more rapidly.

The winds of change are brewing into a storm of change—perhaps a hurricane of change. How can we cope with such change? For me, trees provide a good lesson. If a tree is to withstand a storm, it must be flexible, able to bend with the winds. A rigid tree will soon blow down. In addition, it must have strong roots, be stably anchored in the ground. The same is true for us. If we are to survive the accelerating changes that are coming our way, we need first to be flexible. We need to be able to let go of outdated assumptions and habits of thinking that no longer serve us. We need to find the inner freedom to see things with fresh eyes and respond more creatively. And, second, we need greater inner stability. We need to be stably anchored in the ground of our own being, so that when we meet the unexpected we can remain cool, calm, and collected, not thrown into fear and panic. If we can learn this, then, as I shall be exploring in forthcoming chapters, we will be in a position to respond to the completely unexpected with greater wisdom and maturity.

Crossroads –

Choosing Our Way

No problem can be solved from the same consciousness that created it.

—Albert Einstein

To an extent, the environmental crisis has been inevitable. As soon as we combined the energy of fire with the power of technology, we embarked upon a fateful course. But we did so with the best of intentions. We were applying our unique creativity, first to the task of survival, and then to improving the quality of our lives. Having ensured access to food and shelter, we were seeking a longer, healthier life, in more comfortable conditions. There can be no blame for that.

It is only now, as we realize the many ways in which our best intentions have backfired, that we need to correct our behavior. It is now that we have the opportunity to respond to the crisis we have inadvertently created. Yet the will to respond seems curiously lacking. Instead, we rush headlong toward catastrophe.

The closing pages of Émile Zola's novel, *The Beast in Man*, come to mind. While a train full of soldiers on the way to war is rushing downhill, the driver and the fireman are fighting. The fireman insists on stoking the engine and the driver is trying to stop him. As they tussle, one grabs the other by the throat and together they tumble off the engine, leaving the trainload of drinking and singing soldiers hurtling through the night, totally unaware of what has happened. And there the book ends!

We seem to be in a rather similar situation. We are hurtling at an ever-accelerating pace toward disaster, with no one in the driver's seat. The one significant difference is that we are not unaware of the dangers ahead. It is as if the conductor had walked back through the train announcing that it was out of control, and we still sat playing cards. We hear the bad news, but for one reason or another—perhaps because we are too numbed by the news, feel too powerless, or are too concerned with ourselves—we continue as if it will all turn out fine. Most of us appear more concerned with defending ourselves against our fellow passengers—or with making sure we win our game.

The Will to Change?

We do not lack the science and technology to tackle most of the problems facing us. In almost every area, we know what needs to be done to restore the environment and keep it in a healthy state. Where we do not yet have the necessary means, we know how to begin developing them.

In his 2008 book, *Plan B 3.0*, Lester Brown, president of the Earth Policy Institute in Washington, D.C., paints a comprehensive and rather depressing picture of the planet. Brown offers a masterful summary of the ecological devastation we now face, showing how it will result in economic and political breakdown if these pressures are not handled through the implementation of emergency measures on a global scale. "Plan A," writes Brown, refers to "business as usual," while Plan B is akin to a "wartime mobilization." At its heart is a call to reduce global carbon dioxide emissions eighty percent by 2020. Altogether, Brown calculates that his Plan B—a plan that can in effect save global civilization—would cost the world $190 billion a year. That is quite a lot, yes, but only twenty percent of what the world currently spends on arms in just one year—which is over one trillion dollars! All that we lack is the will.

Are we prepared to reconsider our priorities?

Can we stop destroying the rainforests, now, before it is too late? And who is responsible? Is it the timber-hungry industries, or the hamburger manufacturers who encourage farmers to cut down the forest and use it as pasture for a few years? The governments that allow this to happen? The banks, which demand interest on their loans? Or all of us who in one way or another support the present system?

Can we stop pouring carbon dioxide into the skies, or do we love our energy-hungry lifestyle too much? Can we significantly reduce our use of fossil fuels, or are we too attached to our current technologies and to the comforts they bring?

What will it take for us to change the way we farm the land, to put as much in as we take out? Do the short-term economic and practical effects of such change make it nearly impossible?

What of the "other half" of humanity, who have not yet enjoyed the benefits of "development"? Can we expect them not to want to join the party, especially when at last it seems within their reach? China has now overtaken the U.S. in its consumption of basic resources. At China's current rate of growth, by 2030 it will add another billion cars spewing carbon into the air. And India is not far behind in its consumption trends.

Given such a litany of problems, and the difficulties we face in resolving them, one could be forgiven for thinking that the only thing our ever-accelerating development is taking us toward is unparalleled disaster. Certainly grave dangers lie ahead. But there is also light at the end of the tunnel. And it is toward that light that we are ultimately headed.

To find that light, we must look beyond the many crises now facing us and investigate their underlying cause. Which brings us to the essential question behind all these questions. Why does humanity continue to behave in ways that are clearly not in its best interest? What's wrong with us?

Malady—
A Planetary Cancer

The crew of spacecraft Earth is in virtual mutiny to the order of the universe.

— Edgar Mitchell

How does a species that has developed thinking, reason, foresight, and choice come to behave in such shortsighted ways? We like to think of ourselves as the most intelligent species on this planet, but are we really that intelligent?

How intelligent is a species that understands it is destroying the ecosystem crucial to its existence, and continues to destroy it? Any individual who behaved in such an irrational manner, without any care or respect for their own welfare or that of others, would be classed as insane.

Such behavior has close parallels with cancer. When cancers become malignant, they can grow very fast, with no regard for the rest of the organism. They are part of the body, yet in many respects behave as if they were completely separate. They are also somewhat stupid: if a cancer is successful, it may kill its host, and hence itself.

Similarly, the human population has been growing rapidly and with little regard for its environment. We are a part of the earth's biosphere and totally dependent on it, yet we behave as if we were quite separate from it. Our cities eat into the countryside, eradicating natural ecosystems, spreading deserts of sand and concrete. We allow our toxic wastes to flow into our surroundings, poisoning other species, with hardly a thought. And we too are somewhat stupid; if we continue along this path, we are likely to cause irreversible damage to the biosphere, and will probably destroy ourselves.

But the parallels go deeper than surface appearances and behavior. When we look at what underlies cancer and at what underlies humanity's malignant tendencies, we again find remarkably similar patterns.

In essence, cancer can be thought of as a programming error. The genes in the heart of every cell are essentially a set of chemical programs that provide instructions for the construction of various complex proteins that determine the cell's structure and behavior. Virtually every cell in your body contains the same set of instructions, but for each cell, only those appropriate to that type of cell and its current phase of development are switched on at a given time.

Occasionally, sets of instructions that should be switched off are turned on, or vice versa. This can happen for a number of reasons:

- Radiation from space, nuclear reactors, or medical treatments may damage the control sequences—the switches in the gene.

- Toxic chemicals in the air, in water, or in food may produce changes in the molecular information.

- A virus may enter the cell and insert itself into a gene, disrupting its sequence of instructions.

Guided by an inappropriate set of programs, the damaged cell no longer acts in harmony with the rest of the body. It becomes what is called a *rogue cell*.

Generally, the results are benign. But if instructions to grow and reproduce are turned on, the rogue cells can begin multiplying without limit. This is the beginning of malignancy.

A Virus in the Mind

Humanity's malignant tendencies can likewise stem from an inappropriate set of programs. However, because we have moved on from biological evolution to cultural evolution, the programs that now influence our behavior and development are to be found not in our genes but in our minds. They are our attitudes and values: the way we see life, the way we see ourselves, and what we think is important. It is these, not our genes, that determine most of our decisions and our day-to-day activities.

The biologist Richard Dawkins calls these thought patterns *memes*. The ideas we have about fashion, the values we hold about right and wrong, the beliefs we have about work and leisure, the value we put on money, our assumptions about the purpose of life — these are all memes. Like genes, memes reproduce as they pass from one person to another. A hundred years ago, the meme of using computers to help us in our work did not exist. Today it has spread to everyone; the idea is firmly implanted within us all. Memes are the basic unit of cultural heredity; like the genes in a cell, they bind us together into a cohesive society.

Some memes are useful. Ideas about how to raise children in a loving manner, and reduce the incidence of childhood trauma, are very valuable and can improve the long-term quality of life in a profound way. Others are less useful. A meme that undervalues people of different cultures, races, or classes can spread contempt and strife through society. Such memes are like viruses; they not only spread from one person to another, but can also make society as a whole sick.

This is what lies behind the malignant aspects of modern culture. In much the same way as a virus in the cell can cause programs in the gene to be switched on or off at the wrong time, resulting in cancerous cells, our minds have become infected with a belief system that has switched on memes that might have been useful at an earlier stage in our evolution, but that are totally inappropriate in the modern world. We may, for instance, take the attitude that our own benefit comes before that of others. We may value our material possessions more for the status they bring than for their utility. We may believe that financial or political expediency is more important than our long-term welfare.

It is these outdated mental programs that lie behind much of our self-centeredness, shortsighted decisions, and less-than-intelligent behavior.

How did this happen? Where did this dysfunctional self-interested thinking come from?

Self-Interest –
Misdirected Needs

Happiness belongs to those who are sufficient unto themselves. For all external sources of happiness are, by their very nature, highly uncertain, precarious, ephemeral, and subject to change.

—Arthur Schopenhauer

There is nothing wrong with self-interest as such. We need to take care of our biological selves, make sure we have adequate food, water, and shelter, avoid danger, take rest, and ensure that our other basic needs are met. Without this basic level of self-interest, none of us would survive for very long.

Today, however, we in the more developed countries need to spend very little time and energy fulfilling these physical needs. If we are hungry or thirsty, we simply go to the refrigerator, or we can get in our car and drive down to the supermarket—even in the middle of the night in many cities. We have insulated ourselves from most of the dangers we are likely to encounter in the wild, and provided ourselves with shelters whose level of comfort is far beyond that enjoyed by kings and queens two hundred years ago. If we are still not happy, it is not because we lack some physical need; it is almost certainly because of some inner hunger. We are lacking approval, security, status, power, affection, or the fulfillment of some other psychological need.

This is where the memes come into play. We have been conditioned since birth with the belief that satisfaction of these inner needs comes through our interaction with the world. We seek inner fulfillment through what we have or what we do, through the experiences the world provides, and through the ways others behave toward us. This is the meme that governs so much of our thinking and behavior: the meme that says whether or not we are content with life depends on what we have and what we do.

Prevalent as this meme may be, it seldom provides any lasting satisfaction. A person may gather a great deal of wealth, but is he really more secure? More than likely, he will soon find new sources of insecurity. Are my investments safe? Will the stock market crash? Can I trust my friends? Should I employ "security" companies to protect my possessions?

Someone else, seeking fulfillment through sensory stimulation, may at last find a restaurant with the most exquisite cooking. Does that satisfy her? Or does she wonder, a day later, when she can repeat the experience?

Another may seek fame in order to be approved and accepted. Is he then happy? Or is he upset at having lost the love of his family, or no longer deriving any satisfaction from his work?

Others may believe that if only they could find the right relationship they would be fulfilled. They continually look for the perfect person, the person who satisfies their expectations, the person who will satisfy their inner needs and thus make them happy. Yet such fulfillment can be short-lived. It is usually not long before we start finding imperfections in even the most perfect person.

Part of the problem is that we are looking for fulfillment in a world that is constantly changing. Stock markets go up and down, cars get damaged, fashions come and go, friends change their minds. Consequently, any satisfaction we do gain is likely to be impermanent.

There is, however, a more fundamental reason why this approach does not work. We are responding to our mental needs as if they were bodily needs—as if their cause lay in the world around us. While our bodily needs are a symptom of some physical lack (a lack of food or heat, perhaps), the same is not true of our psychological needs. Most of the time, the cause is in our minds. We feel insecure because we imagine misfortunes that might befall us in the future. Or we feel low self-esteem because we tell ourselves that we are not able to live up to some ideal that we have established for ourselves. There may well be physical causes for our concern—events may not turn out as we would like, we may not be achieving our goals—but, as we will see later, the reason that we feel insecure, unworthy, or whatever, is as much a result of the way we interpret and judge events as it is a result of the events themselves.

Most of the time, we forget that our inner needs have an inner cause. We perceive other people or external circumstance to be the root of our discomfort, and respond as we would to a physical lack— by making adjustments to the physical world. But this only deals with part of the problem. The inner lack continues, and soon reappears in some other guise.

Survival of the Self

The same is true of our need for identity. Most of us derive a sense of self from our experience and interaction with the world. We identify with our personality and our character; with our social status and our job; with our body and our gender; with our nationality, our name, our family; with our beliefs, our education, our interests, our clothes; and even, sometimes, with our car!

Such an identity is forever vulnerable. It has no permanent foundation and is continually at the mercy of events in the world around us. Before long, we find ourselves needing to reassert our sense of self and re-establish who we are, leading to many unnecessary and often undesirable behaviors. Some worry about how they look. Others feel they must constantly defend their character. We may feel insulted if someone forgets our name. We may be proud of our education, and want others to be aware of it. Some of us may argue for hours defending our beliefs. Others may say things they do not believe in order to get attention. We may buy expensive or fashionable clothes, not because we need them, but because they have become part of who we are. And if someone criticizes or insults us, we may not always respond as you might expect a rational, intelligent being to respond.

If this were as far as it went, such behavior would be fairly innocuous. But its consequences spread out into our surroundings. Moreover, when it is augmented by our technology, its repercussions can be very damaging indeed.

The Amplification of Error

Technology amplifies the power inherent in the human hand, and thus amplifies our ability to change the world according to our desires. In the service of our physical needs, this amplification has provided us with great benefits. It has given us plows, irrigation, housing, sanitation, medicine, and heating. But in the service of our inner needs, it has been far from beneficial. Unconsciously assuming that these needs can also be satisfied by changing the world around us, we have applied our creative energies and our technologies to the search for more powerful ways of getting what we think we want. As a result, technology has not only amplified our power to change the world, it has also amplified the errors in our thinking—with potentially disastrous consequences.

It is the demands we make on the world in our relentless search for inner fulfillment that lead us to consume far more than we physically need. No other species consumes more than it needs. This is because no other species has our inner needs, or the means to amplify the demands they create. It is this combination that is causing us to suck the earth dry.

Seen in this light, the nuclear threat, the greenhouse effect, the destruction of the rainforests, the wide-scale extinction of species, soil erosion, the problem of atomic waste, pollution, the energy crisis, the economic crisis, the food crisis, the water crisis, the housing crisis, the sanitation crisis, and the many other crises that humanity faces— all are symptoms of a deeper psychological crisis.

The real crisis is in our thinking, in our perception of what it is we really want and how to go about getting it.

Happiness —
The Mind's Bottom Line

In the final analysis, the hope of every person is simply peace of mind.

—The Dalai Lama

Most of us have become so focused on what we think we want, we have forgotten what it is we are really seeking. We seldom ask ourselves, "What do I really want?" When we go deeply into this question, we find that a common theme lies behind all our desires: We simply want to feel better. We may give this inner feeling different names—joy, happiness, inner peace, satisfaction, fulfillment, bliss, contentment, ease, well-being—but however we describe the quality of mind we seek, the underlying motivation is the same. We are looking to avoid pain and suffering, and to find a more enjoyable state of consciousness.

This is completely natural, and is as true for every other sentient being on this planet as it is for us. It is the organism's way of monitoring how it is doing in life. If there is something amiss—if we need food, for instance—we feel hungry, which is usually an uncomfortable experience. We don't feel good, so, quite naturally, we look for something that will relieve our suffering—in this case, food. Having eaten, we feel better; our lives are in balance again.

This is one thing that unites us all; we all want to reduce our suffering and find a more comfortable, satisfying state of mind.

I may decide to change jobs because I believe I will be happier. I may choose to play table tennis with a friend because I expect to get some pleasure from the game, some good feelings from the exercise, and some satisfaction from winning—or perhaps from seeing my friend win. I may take up hang gliding because I find the challenge enjoyable, or because I get a kick from the release of adrenaline. I may spend time writing a book, forgoing other pleasures, because I gain satisfaction from following my inner drive. If my mind wanders into daydreams, it is probably because they are more entertaining than the task at hand. And I may meditate to feel more at peace within myself.

However, although we may all be looking for a more fulfilling state of mind, our search is not always successful. Sometimes, through shortsightedness or factors beyond our control, we fail to achieve our objectives. At other times, we may get the things we desire, but find they have not made us any happier; they may even have led us to suffer more. How many of us have started a new job, a new course of study, or a new relationship, believing it will make us happy, only to discover later that we were happier with the way things were?

Nor is it always immediate gratification that we are after. We may not enjoy visiting the dentist, but we go in the hope that life will be more enjoyable later. At other times we may worry about the future, creating much discomfort for ourselves, because we unconsciously assume that our worrying will help us avoid future sources of discomfort.

The same principle lies behind our more altruistic actions. We may give up all sense of personal gain and devote time to helping others feel better, perhaps putting ourselves through considerable inconvenience or hardship. But we do it because, at some deeper level, it makes us feel better.

Even the masochist, who sets out to cause himself pain, does so because he gets pleasure from it—or imagines he will.

A more pleasant state of consciousness is the mind's bottom line. It is the fundamental criterion by which, consciously or unconsciously, we make our decisions.

To try to discourage this drive is to miss the point of life. Our error lies not in seeking inner peace, fulfillment, happiness, or joy, but in the ways we set about finding it. Our cultural conditioning has trapped us in a materialist mindset, a meme that says that if we are not happy, something in the world around us has to change.

This is the "virus" that has infected our minds. This is the bug in our thinking that lies at the root of our malignant attitudes and behaviors.

Materialism –
An Addictive Meme

Society is in conspiracy against the manhood of every one of its members. Society is a joint-stock company in which the members agree, for the better securing of his bread to each shareholder, to surrender the liberty of the eater.

—Ralph Waldo Emerson

We have become so successful at molding and manipulating the world that we have come to believe that modifying our surroundings is the way to solve all our problems—not necessarily the only way, but the easiest and simplest way.

For reasons we have already touched on, and will return to later, this approach does not work as well when it comes to our inner

67

needs. But, seduced by the power of our hands and conditioned by past experience, we still try to satisfy them in the way we know best. When this fails to bring any real or permanent satisfaction, we do not question whether our approach may be mistaken. Instead, we try harder to get the world to give us what we want. We buy more clothes, go to more parties, eat more food, try to make more money. Or we give up on these and try different things. We take up squash, buy a video camera, decide to move, or look for new friends. Yet true peace of mind remains as elusive as ever.

We are rather like Nasrudhin, the "wise fool" of Sufi tales, who has lost his key somewhere in his house. But he is searching for it out in the street "because," he says, "there is more light outside." We look for the key to fulfillment in the world around us because that is the world we know best. We know how to change this world, how to gather possessions, how to make people and things behave the way we want—the way we think will bring us happiness. Yet we know much less about our minds and how to find fulfillment within ourselves. There seems to be much less light in there.

A Cultural Trance

From the moment we are born, our culture encourages us to believe that outer well-being is the source of inner fulfillment. As young children, we learn from the example of our elders that it is important to be in control of things, that material possessions offer security, and that doing and saying the right things is the way to gain another person's love. As we grow up, much of our education focuses on knowing the ways of the world so we can better manage our affairs and thus find contentment and fulfillment. And, as we go through life, the daily deluge of television, radio, newspapers, magazines, and billboards reinforces the belief that happiness comes from what happens to us. Wherever we turn, the principle is confirmed, encouraging us to become "human havings" and "human doings" rather than human beings.

Somewhere deep inside, most of us know that this way of operating has its limits. We recognize that whether or not we are content depends as much on how we feel inside ourselves as on how things are around us. We all know people who can remain cheerful when everything seems to be going wrong, who do not get upset at having to wait in a long line, even in the rain. And we hear of more unusual examples—those who have maintained an inner equanimity despite the atrocities of war, or yogis who can sleep peacefully on a bed of nails. The trouble is that our cultural conditioning is so strong that this sort of inner knowing rarely comes to the surface.

Our society has caught itself in a vicious circle. If most of us go through life on the assumption that psychological contentment comes from what we have or do, then that is the message we teach each other. If we see somebody suffering, we are likely to suggest ways they can change the situation in order to feel better. When we want to persuade someone to buy something, we tell them how much happier it will make them. And when our best-laid plans fail to give us what we seek, we encourage each other to try again.

An Exploitative Consciousness

One of the most damaging consequences of looking to the world to satisfy our inner needs is that it results in a competitive mode of consciousness. Perceiving that our surroundings are limited in what they can provide, we compete for the things we believe will bring us happiness: fame, success, friends, promotion, power, attention, and money. Such competition is wasteful in that it leads us to produce things that no one really needs; it also causes us to care less for the earth than we do for our own supposed well-being. In the end, this mentality puts us in competition with Nature herself. This can be seen, for example, in our rampant use of insecticides, herbicides, and fungicides that keep other species at bay so that we can more easily, and more profitably, accomplish our own ends.

This basic operating principle also results in an exploitative mode of consciousness. We use—or perhaps one should say abuse—our surroundings, other people, and even our own bodies in our quest for greater satisfaction. This is the root of our exploitation of the world: the attitudes and values that come from believing that inner well-being is dependent on what we have or do. Money, power, and the other things that people often blame are not the root causes; they are simply symptoms of a deeper underlying error in our thinking.

Addicted to the Material World

We normally think of addiction in terms of drugs, but the effects of our materialist mindset bear all the hallmarks of chemical dependency. Whatever the drug—alcohol, tobacco, coffee, tranquilizers, or some illicit substance—people take it for one simple reason: they want to feel better. They want to feel happy, high, relaxed, in control, free from fear, more in touch with life. In this respect, the drug user is seeking nothing different from anyone else—it is just the way in which he or she is doing it that contemporary society finds unacceptable.

It is the same with our addiction to materialism. We are trying to make ourselves feel better. But any happiness we get is usually only temporary; as soon as one "high" wears off, we go in search of another "fix." We become psychologically dependent on our favorite sources of pleasure—food, music, driving, debating, football, television, sex—whatever it is we get off on (or whatever it is we believe we should get off on). And the ever-present problem of habituation means we need larger and larger doses to achieve the same effect.

This addiction to things is our most dangerous addiction because it is this addiction that underlies the materialism of our age.

If we are to move beyond this precarious phase of our evolution, we must discover how to free ourselves from this addiction. To see what this will entail and where it might lead, we need first to look at some of the effects of this outdated mode of thinking on our personal lives. For it is in our personal lives that we will begin to find the keys to change.

Fear –

The Voice in Our Heads

Fear is not of the present, but only of the past and future.

—A Course in Miracles

Looking to the material world for the satisfaction of our inner needs is the source of much fear. We fear any changes in our circumstances that suggest the world may not be the way we think it ought to be for us to be at peace.

We may fear losing our jobs because of the loss of income and the possibility that our lives may not be so comfortable. We may fear failure for the disapproval it might bring or for the loss of self-esteem. We may fear having nothing to do because we might get bored. We may fear telling the truth because others might not like us for it. We fear the unknown for the dangers it may contain. We fear uncertainty, not knowing whether or not we will find what we are after.

Here lies a sad irony. In the final analysis, what we are all after is a more satisfying state of mind. We want to be happy, at peace within ourselves. Our fears stem from the possibility that the future may bring us greater suffering rather than happiness. Yet the very nature of fear makes us more anxious in the present. And a mind that is anxious cannot, by definition, be a mind that is at peace.

Our concern to avoid suffering in the future keeps us suffering in the present. We have lost the very thing we seek.

Self-Talk

Many of our underlying fears are not so strong that we would label them as actual fears. They may just be concerns, little niggling feelings we have about the way things might turn out. They may not even be conscious concerns; in many cases they surface only in our dreams, in conversation with a friend, or after a couple of drinks.

Nevertheless, however intense or mild they may be, they fill our minds with thoughts. This is our self-talk, the mental chatter we carry on with ourselves. This is the voice inside our heads that comments, often critically, on everything we do. It thinks, "I did that well; people will approve of me." Or it admonishes us, saying, "If only that had not happened, if only I had said it differently, things would have turned out better."

It is the voice that speculates on the future. It thinks, "What if such-and-such were to happen? Would it be good for me?" Or, "What if I buy this? Will it make my life more comfortable?" Or, "Should I make that phone call . . . just in case?"

It wonders what other people are thinking and how they will react. It wonders what might happen to the economy, to housing prices, to our partner, to our lifestyle, to our image, to our car. It worries: "Have I made the right decision?" "Will I have enough money?" "Will I be able to cope?"

This is usually the voice of fear.

This voice in our heads believes its function is to guide us toward greater happiness. But it is the voice of the ego-mind, the part of us that believes that only through what happens to us in the external world can we be at peace within. And since the world around us seldom brings any lasting satisfaction, the ego-mind is always finding more possibilities to fear, new reasons to be anxious.

This is not to imply that we should not think about the future and should not make plans. Our ability to look ahead and gauge the outcome of our actions is one of our most valuable assets. What we do not need is to fill our minds with worry over what may or may not happen. This is not the most constructive use of our imagination or of our intelligence.

Not Now

Besides giving rise to much unnecessary fear, this mental chatter keeps us trapped in time. For as long as we are listening to our internal dialogue, our attention is caught in the past or the future. If half our attention is taken up with the voice in our head, that half is not available for experiencing things as they are, in the present. We don't notice what is going on around us. We don't hear the sounds of birds, the wind, the creaking trees; we don't perceive the mood of our spouse. We don't notice our emotions, or the way our body feels. We are, in effect, only half-conscious.

We have lost the present moment. Lost the *now*.

Saving Time

Similar fears underlie our concern for saving time. We fear that we will not have time to do all the things we think we must do if we are to be content.

So we try to do everything as quickly and efficiently as possible, reducing "unproductive" times such as traveling and shopping to a minimum. Then, we tell ourselves, we will have more time to spend—to spend, that is, on chasing after fulfillment. Time to experience the world in new ways. Time to explore new interests. Time to earn more money—and buy more of the things we think we need.

Little wonder, then, that time is so often equated with money. We apply the same materialist mindset to both. We tell ourselves that the more time we have at our disposal, the greater will be our opportunities to find more happiness. But again we are looking to the future, to the surplus time we will create. Again we miss the enjoyment of the present moment.

Fear of Each Other

Fear also plays havoc with our relationships. We may fear, for example, that our partners or friends may cease to like us, or that they will not as easily understand us as they once did. We may also fear being criticized and judged by them, leading to a fear of rejection.

The list of fears can become lengthy: We might also feel that if they knew what we were really like inside, they would not want to be with us. We may fear the possibility that loved ones or friends will react to us in ways we do not like—for example, ceasing to really listen to us deeply anymore. Further, we may fear that they will not be there when we need them, or somehow prevent us from doing what we really want to do with our lives. And, in turn, how do we react?

- We may not express how we really feel.

- We may not tell the truth.

- We may manipulate others into behaving in the way we want.

- We may think them wrong, blaming them for our fears.

- We may be more concerned with proving that we are right than with hearing their point of view.

- We may attack them in various subtle, or not-so-subtle, ways, looking for ways to make them fear us.

- We may not listen fully. (As soon as we hear something that goes against a cherished belief, the voice in our head tells us where they are wrong and how we should respond—and as long as we are listening to our own self-talk, we are not really listening to them.)

Then we wonder why our relationships can be so full of tensions and problems.

Nor is it just our intimate relationships that suffer. We find things to fear in our friends, our neighbors, our coworkers, and our bosses. We even find things to fear in people we have never met, or may meet once and never again. Will they make me look foolish? Will I be respected and valued? Will they impose on me? Will they ignore me?

Fear also disturbs our relationships with people far away, in other countries. We are afraid of different political systems. We are alarmed by other nations' economic power. We are frightened by their instability. We dread their military might.

Then, as if there were not sufficient fear in the world, we try to diminish our own fear by causing them to fear us. And so the vicious circle grows.

Resisting Change

Not only is fear the root of many of our problems, it also leads us to resist the changes that would help solve our existing problems. Change can threaten our careers, threaten our relationships, threaten our positions, threaten our sense of control, threaten our feelings of security, or threaten our freedom. If this is the way we see change, then it is quite natural for us to resist it. We resist new technologies, new working practices, new customs, new ways of thinking. We resist changes to our plans, changes in our circumstances, and changes in our lifestyles.

Tragically, we also resist the very changes that we most need to make if we are to survive. We resist giving up our cars, reducing our energy consumption, saving water, recycling our waste, and doing without some of the luxuries to which many of us have become accustomed. Stuck with our material addictions, we anticipate that in one way or another the inconveniences of such changes will cause us some discomfort.

The same pattern underlies our resistance to change on a global level. This is why farmers continue to degrade the soil, why corporations continue to buy hardwood from the rainforest, why industries continue to pollute the air and water.

This is why the world continues to spend over a trillion dollars per year on armaments, rather than on food, sanitation, housing, and education. Someone, somewhere, believes the change would not be in their own best interest.

Yet, much as we may resist change, we cannot prevent it. If the patterns of the past hold up (and there is every reason to expect that they will), change is going to come faster and faster. We will need to become more flexible, more free in ourselves, to accept change. To do this, we must learn to let go of our many unnecessary fears.

If we do not, we may well find that fear will be our ruin. For there is one more problem that results from fear, one that we each must take care of if we are to survive an ever-accelerating pace of change. And that is stress.

Stress –

The Wages of Fear

People are disturbed, not by things, but by the view they take of them.

—Epictetus

To the body, fear is a danger signal. The body doesn't stop to determine whether or not the danger is real, or explore how it should respond to the possible danger. As far as it is concerned, there is a potential emergency, and for its own safety it automatically prepares itself for instant action. The heart rate quickens, blood pressure rises, breathing increases, muscles become tense, and the skin begins to sweat, while digestion, reproduction, and other processes that will not be needed for the moment are turned down.

Such a response is very natural, and very valuable. After all, if you were confronted by a wild boar in the woods, or were about to be hit by a bus, you might need to move instantly, and quickly.

But in contemporary society, such physical threats are few and far between. Our mastery of the world has enabled us to avoid or guard against most such dangers, and there are seldom times when we need to prepare ourselves for such instant action. But this does not mean that we are free from threat. Human beings have created a whole new set of things to fear.

Our need to feel in control may be threatened by imposed work-loads, tight deadlines, crowded schedules. We may feel threatened by traffic jams, delayed flights, incompetent staff, unexpected demands, and anything else that might cost us time. Our need for self-esteem, recognition, and approval can be threatened by the fear of failure, the fear of looking foolish in front of others, the fear of criticism, and the fear of being rejected. Uncertainty or anything else that makes us feel insecure can likewise be perceived as a threat.

The trouble is that our bodies respond to these psychological threats just as they would to any physical threat. So we find our hearts thumping, our palms sweating, and our muscles tightening, not be-cause of any physical danger, but because of some danger we per-ceive within our minds—because someone criticizes us, because we have to speak in a group, or because we may be late for a meeting.

The Toll of Stress

Rarely do these psychological threats demand that we run for our lives or fight to the death. There is no physical danger. As far as the body is concerned, it is all a false alarm. So our physiological system then sets about unwinding and recovering. But this is a much slower process. It takes only a second for the body to jump to alert, but it can take many minutes, sometimes even hours, for it to return to a state of ease.

If this occurred only occasionally, there would be no problem. But most of us encounter such inner threats several times a day—sometimes several times an hour—and the body seldom has time to recover from one false alarm before the next one is triggered. Before long, our bodies end up in a permanent state of tension, a permanent state of emergency.

For many of us, this underlying tension is so much a part of contemporary life that we no longer notice it or pay it much attention. But it is still present—a faint background of uptightness, interspersed with periods of high anxiety. Only when we relax fully do we realize just how tense we normally are.

Over a period of time, this background tension begins to affect our thinking, emotions, and behavior. Our judgment deteriorates; we tend to make more mistakes; our perception becomes poorer; we may become depressed, feel hostile toward others, lose our temper more, act less rationally, behave abusively.

Meanwhile, the toll on our bodies is manifested in various ways: aches and pains, indigestion, insomnia, high blood pressure, allergies, lowered immunity, illness, sometimes even premature death.

These are not the only effects of stress. Increased tension, anger, hostility, anxiety, depression, fear, instability, muddled thinking, and selfishness, all damage the general health and well-being of society. This damage contributes to increasing crime, vandalism, violence, terrorism (sanctioned as well as unsanctioned), militarization, war, drug abuse (legal as well as illegal), police harassment, divorce . . . and on and on.

Stress can also have negative effects on our environment. Eighty percent of accidents are caused by "human error," and the more stressed a person is, the more prone they are to error. And the consequences of human error in a nuclear power station, a chemical plant, or a tanker full of crude oil are familiar to us all.

Nor do fatigued and tense people always make the best decisions. More often than not, stress makes us feel more vulnerable, more in need of defending our own interests, more caught up in our ego-mind.

A Disease of the Future

The problem of stress is not likely to go away. As the pace of change continues to increase, the demands on us will also increase. We will have to make more decisions, and faster; have to learn new skills, adapt to new situations, and cope with new threats. As a result, we will find ourselves becoming more tired, making more mistakes, becoming more hostile, more anxious, and more depressed, suffering more ill health, and having more accidents.

If we are to survive in an ever-accelerating world, it is imperative that we learn to cope with the increasing pressures of change without accumulating yet more tension and all its unwanted effects. If we do not, it is more than probable that we will find ourselves sucked into a downward spiral, desperately trying to manage in an increasingly unmanageable world. Breakdowns and burnouts will become the norm. And society will head yet faster toward its own collapse.

The Inner Dimension

Because we are caught in the belief that our inner state is at the mercy of external events, we usually try to manage stress by managing the world. We seek to eliminate or reduce the circumstances that we think are causing our stress. And we seek to minimize the effects that these stresses have on our body and behavior by exercising, eating healthily, or giving the body the rest it needs.

While these may be helpful courses of action, it is also becoming clear that the mind plays a crucial role in most stress reactions. I may, for example, think that being stuck in a traffic jam causes me stress. In doing so, I overlook the crucial role my own thinking plays in my reaction. It is not the traffic jam itself that is causing the tension. A traffic jam is actually quite relaxing. No activity is called for, no vigilance is required, there is nothing that needs to be controlled, nobody coming along to interrupt my thoughts. In many respects, it is the sort of situation I may have been wishing for all day. I can shut my eyes and come to no harm.

If I find such a situation stressful, it is because of what I am telling myself—that voice in the head again. I may be imagining the possible negative consequences of being delayed, or be angry with myself for not having chosen a better route. I may be saying that this is not what I expected, that I want the situation to be different from the way it is. It is my thoughts that make me upset, not the jam itself.

Someone else who remains relaxed in a jam may be glad to be away from the demands of telephones, papers to sign, questions to answer, disagreements to settle. She may be pleased to have to miss the meeting. Or she may realize that there is nothing she can do to change the situation, so she may as well arrive late and relaxed as late and upset.

In almost all cases, it is not the situation itself that causes stress, but the way we perceive the situation. If I see the situation as a threat to what I want, a threat to my sense of identity, a threat to my inner well-being, a threat to my getting what I believe I need in order to be happy, or a threat to my expectations of how things should be, then I may well cause myself stress.

Managing the Mind

This alternate way of seeing a situation is the new meme that we must adopt if we are to survive the consequences of ever-accelerating change. The old meme tells us: The way you feel inside is a reflection of what is going on in the world around you—what you have, what you do, what you experience. The new meme says: The way you feel inside is a reflection of the way you perceive the world. *If you want to feel more at peace in yourself, don't try to change the world around you, for that can only bring temporary relief at best; change your judgments and interpretations about the world—change your mind.*

Adopting this meme actually gives us much greater control over our inner responses. We may not always have much influence over the situation we find ourselves in, but the way in which we perceive a situation is something over which we have a great deal of influence. We always have a choice as to whether we see a change as a threat or as an opportunity. Thus, we always have a choice as to whether or not we upset ourselves over things.

This is not to imply that we should never try to change the world; there may be many things we can do to make the world a better place. But we should not fall into the trap of believing that this is the path to our personal inner fulfillment.

Nor does it mean we should sit back and let the world walk all over us. There may be many things we can do that will relieve the pressure we are under. If, for instance, we find ourselves suffering from an excessive workload, we can look for ways to reduce that particular problem. But what we do not need to do is make ourselves upset, and possibly ill, in the process. In fact, we will probably respond with more insight, higher creativity, clearer direction, better poise, and more effectiveness if our minds are not hampered by a response more appropriate to our evolutionary past.

Learning to manage our own thinking and perception is more than a very practical means of managing stress—with all the consequent benefits that may have for us as individuals and as a species. As we learn to work with ourselves in this way, we are learning to free ourselves from fear. We are beginning to challenge some of the fundamental beliefs that control our lives and that lead us to behave in shortsighted ways that are seldom in our true best interest.

The
Awakening

Not I, not I, but the wind that blows through me!
A fine wind is blowing the new direction of Time.
If only I let it bear me, carry me, if only it carry me!
If only I am sensitive, subtle, Oh delicate, a winged gift!
If only, most lovely of all, I yield myself and am borrowed
By the fine, fine wind that takes its course through the chaos of the
    world
Like a fine, an exquisite chisel, a wedge-blade inserted;
If only I am keen and hard like the sheer tip of a wedge
Driven by invisible blows,
The rock will split, we shall come at the wonder, we shall find the
    Hesperides.
Oh, for the wonder that bubbles into my soul;
I would be a good fountain, a good well-head,
Would blur no whisper, spoil no expression.

      What is the knocking?
      What is the knocking at the door in the night?
      It is somebody wants to do us harm.
      No, no, it is the three strange angels.
        Admit them, admit them.

—D. H. Lawrence,
The Song of a Man Who Has Come Through

Dehypnosis –
Breaking the Trance

The first problem for all of us, men and women,
is not to learn, but to unlearn.

—Gloria Steinem

In the preceding chapters, we have considered how humanity's preoccupation with material progress and outer achievement can be seen as a form of cultural conditioning. The values imparted to us through our upbringing, education, and social experience have seduced us into accepting a set of assumptions about what is important, what we need, and what will bring us fulfillment. As a result, we behave as if inner peace and happiness come from what we have and do.

Most of us can see the fallacy in this approach. We know that whether or not we remain calm in a particular situation depends as much on how we perceive and interpret events as on the events themselves. But our conditioning is so pervasive that for much of the time our inner knowing remains hidden.

The Hidden Observer

A parallel phenomenon occurs in ordinary hypnosis. In an experiment conducted at Stanford University by one of the pioneers of hypnosis research, Dr. Ernest Hilgard, a subject was told that his left hand would feel no pain when placed in a bucket of ice-cold water. Anyone who has ever experienced ice-cold water will know that it can be very painful indeed, yet the subject reported that he felt fine; there was no pain. The hypnosis, it would seem, had been successful.

The subject was then asked to allow his right hand to engage in some "automatic writing"—that is, without looking, to let the hand simply write anything it wanted. He wrote: "It's freezing." "Ouch." "It hurts." "Take my hand out." Although the hypnosis had elicited the desired behavior, apparently it had not been able to override a deeper level of truth.

Hilgard called the unhypnotized part of the mind, the part that still felt the pain, the "hidden observer." One of his subjects described it as "the part of me that looks at what is, and doesn't judge it." Another said it was "more like my real self, only more objective. When I'm in hypnosis, I'm imagining, letting myself pretend, but somewhere the hidden observer knows what's really going on."

The same would seem to happen with our search for a more satisfying state of mind. The hidden observer within us knows that the key to fulfillment lies within. Yet this knowledge rarely comes to the surface and most of us continue to "pretend" that outer well-being is the best path to inner fulfillment.

Until, that is, we engage in some automatic writing (or "channeling," as some call it), during which we may find ourselves expressing truths we did not know we knew. Our hidden observer may reveal itself in other ways. It may speak to us in our dreams in the form of images symbolic of our inner knowing. We may recognize the folly of our ways in times of deep reflection. Or, liberated from our conditioned responses by a glass or two of wine, we may temporarily glimpse the inanity of the games we play.

It is as if a voice is there within us, aching to be heard, but unable to get past the clamor of our conditioned thinking. The self-talk of the ego-mind is so busy describing what is happening, judging whether it is good or bad for us, and telling us what we should think and do, that there is little opportunity for our inner knowing to be heard. Instead, we remain attached to our illusions, dreaming of the fulfillment we believe they will bring.

Clinical Versus Cultural Hypnosis

If we are to deal with the root cause of the crises now confronting us, we must awaken from our trance and regain a fuller contact with our own inner wisdom. We need the cultural equivalent of dehypnosis. But while waking from ordinary hypnosis is a simple matter—the hypnotist may count to three, snap his fingers, and simply tell you to wake up—awakening from our cultural trance is not nearly so easy.

To start with, there is no hypnotist standing by our side to awaken us. Most of our conditioning occurred long ago, much of it before we could speak or remember. It has come through many different sources: parents, teachers, friends, strangers, books, magazines, radio, television, films, advertising. It is part of the fabric of our society. No single person was responsible.

Another very important difference between clinical and cultural hypnosis concerns the depth of the conditioning. In his book *Waking Up*, the psychologist Charles Tart shows that ordinary hypnosis is a voluntary and limited relationship between consenting adults. The power given to the hypnotist is limited by time (usually to an hour or two) and by various ethical constraints (the subject does not expect to be bullied, threatened, or harmed). If the hypnosis does not work very well, the subject is not blamed. And, although profound changes may occur for a short while, no basic or long-term shifts in personality or "reality" are expected by the subject—other than, perhaps, the relinquishing of some unwanted habit.

With our cultural conditioning, the situation is the opposite:

▸ Our consensus trance is not voluntary; it begins at birth, without our conscious agreement.

- All authority is surrendered to the parents, family members, and other caretakers, who initially are regarded as omniscient and omnipotent.

- Induction is not limited to short sessions; it involves years of repeated reinforcement.

- Clinical therapists would consider it highly unethical to use force, but our cultural hypnotists often do: a slap on the wrist or a severe reprimand for misbehaving. Or perhaps more subtle, but equally powerful, emotional pressures: "I will love you only if you think and behave as I tell you."

- Finally, and most significantly, the conditioning is intended to be permanent. It may come from the very best of intentions, but it is, nevertheless, meant to have a lasting effect on our personalities and on the way we evaluate the world.

This is why awakening from our cultural trance entails far more than a simple snapping of the fingers. There is a lifetime's worth of extremely powerful induction to be overcome.

We would seem to be firmly stuck with our conditioning. Indeed, most of the time we are. Yet there are occasions when we do wake up and see things in a different light. In those moments, we are given a glimpse of what is possible.

Presence —
The Timeless Moment

"Are you a God?" they asked the Buddha. "No," he
  replied.
"Are you an angel, then?" "No."
"A saint?" "No."
"Then what are you?"
Replied the Buddha, "I am awake."

—Houston Smith

Many of us can remember times when we have been blessed with a taste of self-liberation. The trigger may have been some spectacular scenery, a touching encounter, the birth of a child, or a moment of tenderness. Whatever the reason—and sometimes there is no apparent reason—we are taken out of ourselves and see things without the layers of judgment and concern that usually cloud our minds. In the words of the visionary poet William Blake, the doors of perception are cleansed and we see things as they are—infinite.

In those special moments, we feel more aware, more fully in the present, no longer lost in thoughts and concerns. There is a sense of liberation, a release from the humdrum affairs of the world. Perhaps there are feelings of awe and wonderment, a deeper connection with ourselves, with others, with nature, and sometimes with the whole of creation. We may remember what it is to be fully alive. In those moments, we are free. We are truly at ease.

Countless examples of such moments of grace are to be found in autobiographies, poetry, and spiritual literature all over the world. Here is one from the historian Kenneth Clark:

> It took place in the church of San Lorenzo, but did not seem to be connected with the harmonious beauty of the architecture. I can only say that for a few minutes my whole being was irradiated by a kind of heavenly joy, far more intense than anything I had known before. . . . That I had "felt the finger of God" I am quite sure, and, although the memory of this experience has faded, it still helps me to understand the joys of the saints.

Margaret Isherwood recalled an experience she had when she was nine years old:

> Suddenly the Thing happened, and as everybody knows, it cannot be described in words. The Bible phrase, "I saw the heavens open" seems as good as any if not taken literally. I remember saying to myself, in awe and rapture, "So it's like this; now I know what heaven is like, now I know what they mean in church."

The Indian poet Rabindranath Tagore was watching the sun rise in a Calcutta street when

> suddenly, in a moment, a veil seemed to be lifted from my eyes. . . . The thick cloud of sorrow that lay on my heart in many folds was pierced through and through by the light of the world. . . . There was nothing and no one whom I did not love at that moment.

And Warner Allen, in his book *The Timeless Moment*, describes a flash of illumination that occurred during a performance of

Beethoven's Seventh Symphony. Again, he found his experience hard to describe:

> A dim impression of the condition of the objective self might be given by a jumble of incoherent sentences. "Something has happened to me—I am utterly amazed—can this be that? (*That* being the answer to the riddle of life)—but it is too simple—I always knew it—it is remembering an old forgotten secret—like coming home—I am not 'I,' not the 'I' I thought—there is no death—peace passeth all understanding."

Common to the majority of such experiences is the fact that they come unbidden. "I did nothing to make it happen." "It came upon me." In such moments, waking up seems effortless.

Two Sides of a Fence

The realities of our day-to-day waking consciousness and of these moments of liberation are so different that it is almost as if a mental fence divided the two. On one side of the fence, I am caught in my mind—in my thoughts, my anxieties, my judgments, and my fears. I may on occasion recognize that this is all unnecessary, and that it removes me from the present moment, but such passing insights are seldom sufficient to release my mind from the grip of my conditioning. So deeply ingrained is my attachment to what I believe I should be thinking and doing, there seems no way over that fence. Indeed, for much of the time I have totally forgotten there is another way of being.

But when, for one reason or another, I find myself on the other side of the fence, it all seems so simple. It is clear that I need do nothing to feel at ease and at peace. I know I am at peace. And I know that nothing can threaten this peace, for it is an intrinsic quality of life itself, not something that can be created or destroyed. It seems obvious that all I need do is relax and simply let go of my fears. How, I wonder, could I ever have gotten myself so muddled and entangled?

In this state of consciousness, the true meaning of nonattachment is apparent. It is not, as it is often interpreted to be, a withdrawal from life—a lack of concern, a lack of responsibility, or a lack of feeling. It is simply that I am no longer attached to the need for things or events to be a certain way. I have let go of the belief that what goes on around me determines whether or not I am content. In this state, I am free to respond to the needs of others without the aura of self-concern that troubles so much of our thinking. Mahatma Gandhi put it very clearly:

> Detachment is not apathy or indifference. It is the prerequisite for effective involvement. Often what we think is best for others is distorted by our attachment to our opinions: we want others to be happy in the way we think they should be happy. It is only when we want nothing for ourselves that we are able to see clearly into others' needs and understand how to serve them.

Timeless Wisdom

Gandhi's ideas were not new. His philosophy was drawn from the *Bhagavad Gita*, one of India's ancient spiritual texts. The reason we are confused and suffer, says the *Gita*, is that we are caught in the conflicts that arise from attachment to the fruits of our actions. Our motivations are colored by our unfulfilled inner needs, which lead to a personal investment in things turning out a certain way. The wise, on the other hand, are free from such concerns; they do not laugh or cry at the ups and downs of the world, but maintain an inner equanimity in the face of loss or gain.

In one way or another, this is what all the great religions have been trying to tell us: They may couch it in different terms, clothe it in different doctrines, teach it through different metaphors, and approach it through different practices, but they all share the same underlying goal. That goal is to leave behind self-centered desires—to be free from our attachment to material circumstances and from our beliefs about the way things should or should not be. It is to rise above suffering. It is to open ourselves to a higher wisdom and reconnect with the essence of life. It is to regain our vitality.

The essence of such teachings is not determined by time or culture, although these may influence its form and expression. It is determined by the essential nature of the mind. And that is the same now as it was five thousand years ago.

Back to the Present

There is another sense in which this wisdom is "timeless." It is the undoing of our "timefulness." It offers release from our bondage to past and future, and a return to the serenity of the present moment.

The thirteenth-century Christian mystic Meister Eckhart described the way, in moments of inner quiet,

> there exists only the present instant . . . a Now which always and without end is itself new. . . . There is no yesterday nor any tomorrow, but only Now, as it was a thousand years ago and as it will be a thousand years hence.

And six hundred years later, Richard Jefferies wrote:

> It is eternity now, I am in the midst of it. It is about me in the sunshine; I am in it, as the butterfly in the light-laden air. Nothing has to come; it is now. Now is eternity; now is immortal life.

In some senses, of course, we are always in the present. Our past we know from memories, but those memories are experienced in the present, just as our future is something we imagine in the present. Whatever we may be thinking and doing, we are doing it *now*. Even when we are totally absorbed in thoughts about the past or the future, the thoughts themselves are occurring in the "now."

When we say we are not in the present, we really mean that the *object of our attention* is not in the present. We are looking back to the past or forward to the future. To return to the present is to return our attention to what is going on here and now.

The mind that is attending to the present is a mind that is free from distracting self-talk about what has or has not happened or what might or might not happen.

A mind in the present moment is free to experience *what is*. This does not imply that one no longer takes any notice of the past nor considers the future. There is still much to learn from the past, and there are still innumerable ways we can influence the future and thus improve the quality of our lives and the lives of others. The difference is that, once liberated from its state of trance, the mind is no longer lost in fruitless concerns about things that happened in the past, nor is it caught up in anxieties about what may or may not happen in the future. Instead, we can focus more fully on the task at hand because the energy of attention is now more available.

Moreover, a mind that is free from worry and concern is—almost by definition—a mind that is at peace. Here, in the present moment, we find what we have been seeking all along. It is not "out there" in some circumstance or thing, but right here within us, at the core of our being.

There is nothing we have to do or achieve to find inner peace, joy, and fulfillment. All that is needed is to remove the layers of thought that have kept it hidden, to stop worrying about whether or not we are ever going to find it in the future; and to realize that it is— as it always has been and always will be—here now.

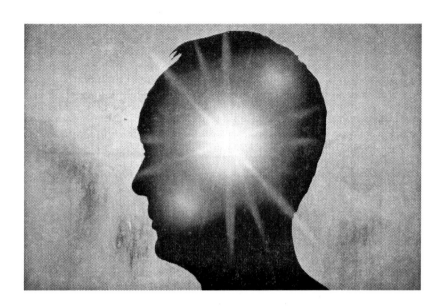

Enlightenment –
A New Way of Seeing

If being right is your goal,
    you will find error in the world,
    and seek to correct it.
But do not expect peace of mind.
If peace of mind is your goal,
    look for the errors in your beliefs and expectations.
    Seek to change them, not the world.
And be always prepared to be wrong.

Being able to experience reality as it is, undistorted by our hopes and fears, is often referred to as *enlightenment*. The *light* in *enlightenment* is usually thought of in the sense of illumination. A mind that

95

is enlightened is said to be an *illumined* mind; it is a mind that has "seen the light," or sees things in a new light.

There is, however, another sense of the word *enlighten* that is equally appropriate—what we might call "a lightening of the load."

The heaviest burdens in this life are not our physical burdens but our mental ones. We are weighed down by our concern for the past and our worries about the future. This is the load we bear, the weariness that comes from our timefulness.

To en-lighten the mind is to relieve it of this load. An enlightened mind is a mind no longer weighed down by attachments; it is a mind that is *free*.

Being free, it is a mind that is no longer so serious about things; it takes things more lightly.

Could this be why enlightened people often laugh and smile more?

A Shift in Perception

From either perspective, that of illumination or that of lightening the load, the essence of enlightenment is a shift in perception. It is a shift from seeing the world through the eyes of anxiety to seeing without judgment—seeing what is rather than what ought to be or might be.

Enlightenment is waking up to the illusions contained in the belief we have been fed since birth: the familiar belief that whether or not we are at peace depends upon what we have or do in the material world. It is discovering for oneself, as a personal experience of life, that whether or not we are at peace depends on our perception and interpretation of events.

This alternative way of seeing is to be found at the core of most of the great spiritual traditions. It is, for instance, the very foundation stone of Buddhism. As a prince in a wealthy kingdom, the young Buddha—Siddhartha, as he was then called—had everything he could wish for in the material world. But, like many of us today, he realized that wealth and luxury do not in themselves remove suffering. So he left the palace and set out, determined to find a way to end suffering. After six years of studying with various ascetics, yogis, and other holy men, and learning many practices and mental disciplines, he was scarcely nearer his goal. Then one day, sitting in meditation, he had an insight that caused him to wake up—and hence to gain the name *Buddha,* which simply means "the awakened one."

He summarized his realization in the Four Noble Truths, which might be paraphrased as follows:

1. We all experience suffering in one way or another—mental, physical, emotional, spiritual.

2. We create our own suffering. It is a consequence of our desiring things to be other than they are.

3. It need not be this way. We have a choice as to how we perceive the world and live our lives.

4. There are systematic ways to go about changing how we think and perceive.

Parallel ideas can be found in Christianity. The admonition "Sinners repent, for the Kingdom of Heaven is at hand" is often interpreted as telling us to be sorry for what we have done, because the day of judgment is coming. But if we look back to the Greek texts, we find another possible interpretation.

The Greek word that we translate as "sin" is *amartano*. This, as Maurice Nichol has pointed out in his book *The Mark*, is a term derived from archery and means to have missed the mark, to have missed the target. The target we are each seeking is inner fulfillment, but, imagining that it will come from what we have or do, we aim in the wrong direction, and thus "miss the mark." It is this fundamental error as to how to find happiness and peace of mind that is our "original sin." The word translated as "repent" is *metanoia*, which means a transformation of mind. So "Sinners repent" can also be translated as "You who have missed your target, and not found happiness in the world around you, change your thinking," for what you are looking for lies very close by, within you.

Nor is it only religious teachers who have proclaimed this truth. The Greek philosopher Epictetus, living in the first century A.D., gave one of the most succinct and powerful expositions of this wisdom when he wrote, "People are disturbed, not by things, but by the view they take of them."

Choosing to See

In principle, we can make this shift of perception at any time we choose. Whenever we are caught up in trying to make the future the way we want it to be—which, in one way or another, is most of the time—we have the opportunity to look at things differently. Rather than wondering, "How can I get such-and-such so that I can be happy?" we could ask, "Even if I were to get what I want, would I then be at peace?" And, "If I do not get what I want, can I still be at peace?"

If we have a willingness to look at things differently, the answers to these questions are nearly always "No" and "Yes," respectively. Then, having let go of our anxiety about the future in the wake of our recognition that such anxiety is useless, we find that our attention is once again free to return to the here and now.

That much is easy. The difficulty comes in remembering to stop and ask. It is in this area that we need practice. And for most of us, the aspect of life that offers us the most opportunity for practice—and the one in which we most need help—is our personal relationships. For it is here that we come up against some of our deepest conditioning and some of our strongest judgments.

Relationships—
The Yoga of the West

The only person who behaves sensibly is my tailor. He takes my measure anew every time he sees me. All the rest go on with their old measurements.

—George Bernard Shaw

The contemporary sage Ram Dass once remarked that "relationships are the yoga of the West." This does not mean our relationships should involve sitting or standing in strange positions; physical yoga is only one kind of yoga. The Sanskrit word *yoga* means "union," and a *yoga* is any path that leads to union, a union with the cosmos and with one's own inner essence—in other words, a path to spiritual awakening.

Our personal relationships offer us such a path because they can bring into focus those shortcomings in our thinking and behavior we have already examined. We have already broached the fact that most of us have experienced the rather unloving behavior to which our relationships can lead:

* Hiding our thoughts and feelings as well as our past actions.

* Trying to prove we are better in some way.

* Fighting to prove some belief or point of view.

* Manipulating others so they will behave as we want.

* Being not ourselves, but the way our partner would like us to be.

* Saying things we do not believe in the hope of winning approval.

Such patterns stem from the conditional nature of our love. We saw earlier how we create anger, resentment, and stress for ourselves when we think someone is preventing us from finding peace or joy in life. With conditional love, the same process operates in reverse.

When we judge that someone may help us in our search for fulfillment, we feel good about them. When they appear to match our picture of the perfect person—the person who will make us wonderfully happy—we love them.

But such love is highly conditional: It depends on the way a person behaves, the way they look, the values they profess, and perhaps the feelings they have for us. We love them for their appearance, their manner, their mind, their body, their talents, their smell, their dress, and (if they agree with our own) their beliefs and values. The more they match our expectations of the perfect person, the more we love them.

Such love turns the other person into someone special—someone who in our eyes shines out above others. We have judged them to be fascinating, wise, kind, honest, good-looking, sexy, humorous, artistic, intelligent, understanding, or whatever else appeals to our egomind. We have judged them to be someone who will satisfy our needs and desires.

Then, in order that the one we "love" stays around and delivers the fulfillment we seek, we play the same game in reverse. We try to match their needs and expectations. We do and say the right things and try to be the right kind of person—clever, witty, sincere, strong, caring, or whatever else we think they want. We want to be their special person, the one they want to be with.

But such love is very fragile. Should our partner not do as we wish, or otherwise fail to meet some dream we have of them, we can easily find ourselves slipping into the opposite reaction. Fear or even hate raises its head once again and we find ourselves becoming upset with them and falling out of love.

If we are not very careful—and usually most of us are not—our partner's failure to meet our expectations is interpreted by us as an unjustified attack. And a too hasty response on our part can lead us into unnecessary and frequently disruptive behaviors. We may try to defend ourselves, perhaps by responding with an attack or by criticizing them in some way. We may withdraw our affection, withholding what they need. We may try to make them feel guilty, in the hope that they will change and once more satisfy our needs. We may even wonder what we saw in them in the first place.

But if they are as inwardly vulnerable as we are (which is very likely), they may well perceive our reaction as an equally unjustified attack on them. If they are not careful, they are likely to find themselves responding in similar ways. All too easily, we and our partner have become caught in a vicious circle of resentment and blame.

Little wonder that many such relationships break down.

Damaging as such reactions may be, we can also turn them to good effect. Our disagreeable responses and less welcome behavior can, if we care to look, reveal our inner vulnerabilities. They can help us become aware of our hidden fears; and by exploring what is going on, we can begin to see some of the psychological attachments we have formed. Each painful reaction becomes an opportunity to grow and mature—and to return to the present moment.

Seen in this light, our personal relationships can become our *yoga*: a path from self-centeredness toward self-liberation.

Judgment

If our thinking is ruled by the belief that inner peace, joy, and contentment come from what we have or do in the world, we may find ourselves treating other people as we do material things. We look to them for satisfaction of our inner needs, and thus judge them according to whether we think they may help or hinder us in our search for personal fulfillment. I might judge an inflexible bureaucrat who causes me considerable inconvenience and stands in the way of my getting what I want as "selfish" or "uncaring." Conversely, if one goes out of his way to assist me, I might judge him as "kind" and "friendly."

In general terms, if we like the person and think they are on our side, we categorize them as a "good" person. Conversely, if we dislike them or think they stand in the way of our fulfillment, we are liable to put them in the category of "bad" people—those who need improvement.

Such judgments are projections of our own mind, our own hopes and fears. Someone else, with different hopes and different fears, might see the same person in another light. How many times have we been surprised to find someone dislikes a person we think highly of, or, conversely, likes a person we have judged to be a waste of time?

Since such judgments are of our own making, and they may bear no relation to the truth. For all I know, the inflexible bureaucrat may have been preoccupied with a domestic crisis and may later have regretted the way he treated me. Conversely, the more amenable person may have been trying to manipulate me for his own ends.

There is a big difference between this sort of judgment and the evaluations we might make of a person's skills, character, behavior, or other personal attributes. If you are interviewing someone for a position in a company, you need to judge their suitability for the job. Do they have the necessary skills and experience? How will they respond under pressure? Are they trustworthy? Will they fit in with the culture? Such judgments are very valuable. We need to be good judges of character, or to weigh up a situation and judge the best course of action. Judgment in the sense of discernment is most important.

But to judge another person's worth as a human being is never justified. We may like or dislike their appearance, personality, or beliefs, but this has no bearing on their value as a being. We have no right to make such judgments. No person has any greater or lesser value than any other person.

Not only are such judgments not justified; they are not very helpful. They keep us from seeing the other person in the present moment. Instead, we see them through the eyes of the past and through our concerns for the future. We do not see them as they really are.

Letting Go of Judgments

Think of a friend. Anyone will do: either gender, any age. The first person who comes into your mind will serve perfectly well.

Pause for a moment and consider the thoughts you have about them. Consider their looks . . . the way they dress . . . their habits . . . the way they speak . . . and anything else that comes to mind about them.

Notice the feelings you have toward them.

Consider the various things that you like about this person. What makes them a friend?

Notice those things that you do not appreciate so much, the changes that would improve them in your eyes.

Then pause to remember that all these thoughts are based on past experience. You are projecting the past onto that person. You are not actually appreciating them as they are today.

Now (and this may take a little more time) take one of these thoughts, recognize that it has been derived from past impressions, and ask, "Is that how this person really is? Is that how they experience themselves? Is this how others see them? Or is it simply a picture I have made of them—a picture I have projected onto them?"

Ask this about the various other thoughts you have about this person, trying each time to step beyond your interpretations and really see them as they are.

You will probably discover that the more you let go of your projections and perceive the other person with a more open mind, the more you begin to understand them. As you understand them, you begin to accept them as they are; and then, you may notice a deeper sense of closeness. You are beginning to perceive them with a more open heart—with more empathy and compassion.

You can do the same exercise focusing on someone you do not know so well. As you let go of preconceptions about who and how they might be, a new degree of openness can appear. You begin to understand what it really means to love a stranger—or even to love an enemy. It is not a romantic love or an infatuation; it is a love of compassion based on the simple acceptance of another being just as they are.

You may also try the exercise with yourself as the focus. From this you may discover that loving yourself is not simply a matter of thinking how wonderful you are; it is also letting go of all the judgments you may have of yourself, and accepting yourself with greater compassion.

Love and Judgment

We have already seen two ways in which the materialist meme—the belief that inner peace, joy, and fulfillment depend on what we have or do in the external world—can limit us. It prevents us from being at peace. And it takes our attention away from the present moment. We are now seeing a third way in which it can be a handicap. It can stand in the way of love.

Love, whether it be the love of a child for its mother, the love of two lovers for each other, or the love of nature, is born of a sense of oneness. It is an expression of a deeper sense of connection. And its goal is unity—to be one with that which one loves.

When we judge another person, we see the ways in which their thoughts, words, and deeds—and by implication their feelings, desires, and goals—differ from our own. In our minds, we experience separation rather than oneness. Such separation is the opposite of love.

Love –

The Gift of Peace

Love is not something you do,
Love is a way of being.
And more than that.
It is simply being,
Being with another person, however they may be.
Holding no judgments, having no agendas,
No desire to control,
No need to prove your love,
No intrusion upon their soul.
Nothing but a total acceptance of their being,
Born of your acceptance of yours.

Unconditional love is not unconditional approval of another's actions, irrespective of their effects on others. It is unconditional love of the being behind the actions. It does not depend on the way a person thinks, feels, or behaves. It does not pause to assess whether or not another is worthy of affection. It recognizes that beneath all our various appearances and activities, we all want to feel loved. In this, we are all united.

Unconditional love recognizes that we are all, to some extent, caught in the belief that our inner satisfaction is determined by what goes on around us. We all feel the need for security, control, recognition, approval, and stimulation to varying degrees; we all feel threatened from time to time by things that seem to stand in the way of our fulfillment; and we can all make mistakes.

The Love of God

This love is the love of which the great religions have spoken—the love of God. If God (and each of us has our own interpretation of that word) exists and loves us, it is not because of something we have done. God does not judge us as good or bad. Such judgments stem from our own needs, not God's.

Nor does the love of God depend on how earnestly we worship God. That is merely another projection of our needs. The love of God is a love for our being, for the inner essence that dwells within us all.

This is the love each of us seeks. And this is the way we want others to love us. We want to be loved just as we are, warts and all.

Moreover, it is the way we would prefer to love others. To know the love of God is to have unconditional love in our own hearts. We want to be able to love in this way because inside we know that it is more lasting and more deeply satisfying than any conditional love.

But how do we attain such a love? That is the eternal challenge. How do we learn to love our neighbor as we love ourselves?

Forgiveness

The best neighbor we can practice the art of loving with is the neighbor we are already in close relationship with, the person we share ourselves most intimately with. Whatever each of us is thinking, saying, or doing, we always have one thing in common. Each and every one of us wants to feel loved and at peace within.

It is easy to forget this. When we do, we may find ourselves thinking the other person has said or done something bad. That is when we should try to step back for a moment and appreciate that they too, in their own way, are looking for love and seeking to find some peace in this ever-changing world. Where we differ is in how we go about satisfying this quest. When others try to find peace and love in ways that appear to conflict with our own attempts to find fulfillment, we may feel angry or frustrated or frightened or resentful or distant or some other less-than-loving emotion.

Forgiveness is letting go of the belief that the other person did wrong. It is not saying, "I know you committed a sin, but I will not hold it against you." It is a recognition that we are all seeking the same goal, but caught as we all are in our ego-mind, we may act in ways that are shortsighted, self-centered, and not in the best interests of other people. Forgiveness is acknowledging that I, too, given the same history and circumstances, could easily have made a similar mistake.

The same sentiment is expressed in the New Testament. The Greek word that we translate as "forgiveness," *aphesis*, means "to let go." And, as we saw earlier, the Greek word for "sin" means "to miss the mark," to be seeking inner fulfillment in the wrong places. To forgive others their sins is to recognize that they have merely missed the mark. It is to let go of the judgment that they have wronged us, and to recognize instead that they are just as caught up in illusions as we are.

Forgiveness is also a letting go of the belief that another person has upset us. It is to take responsibility for our feelings of distress, and recognize that whatever the other person may have done or not done, the feelings we have are our own creation.

This was brought home to me very clearly several years ago, when I discovered that a business associate had been lying to me about progress on a project we were working on. What made it worse was the fact that I had already expressed to him my feeling that he was being less than honest; he had told me not to worry, that he was indeed telling me the truth. When the truth finally did emerge, I was livid—not so much because the deal had fallen through, which in itself was a blow, but more because, despite his promises, he had been lying to me all along.

Two weeks later, I was still upset—so much so that merely thinking of him late at night created sufficient distress to prevent me from going to sleep for another hour or two. Then I realized something: He was not doing anything to me *now*. If I was angry now, it was my own responsibility. I was creating feelings of anger and hostility from the thoughts I was having. There was a conflict between the situation at hand—what I call the "what is"—and what I think "should be." In this case, the "should" was that when someone *promises* you they are telling you the truth, then they should do so. It was this that was upsetting me. There was a conflict between my personal values and the fact that someone else had not lived up to them.

As I began to explore the issue more fully, I put myself in his shoes. I saw that here was another human being, struggling to get by in life, who, for one reason or another (who knows what had happened to him in the past?), had tried to alleviate a difficult situation by not telling me the truth. And the deeper he'd gotten into the mess, the more he'd been forced to keep up the pretense. This is not to say that I thought his actions acceptable, or that I pushed my own values aside. I still hold that if someone promises that they are telling the truth, then they should. Most of us hold this value; that's why we ask people to swear under oath, and why we consider perjury a serious crime. But I could understand how he had gotten himself into that situation; and from that understanding came forgiveness.

I did not make him right, or absolve him of his unacceptable behavior. But I did stop making myself upset. I was free to sleep at night in relative peace.

When anger arises, it is real. And we should not suppress it. That is only likely to make us stressed and sick. But we do not need to carry the anger around with us long after the event. Holding onto grievances only results in an unnecessary disturbance of our inner peace.

Practicing Forgiveness

Forgiveness is not an easy practice. As anyone who has walked this path knows, it requires commitment, vigilance, and patience.

It also requires continual self-reminding. Once someone or something has triggered one of our inner vulnerabilities, it is all too easy to forget our higher goal. We forget our practice—only to remember later how we could have seen things differently.

On those occasions when we do remember that it is our interpretation of events that determines our reaction, we can help ourselves by pausing to ask our "hidden observer" whether it can suggest another way of seeing the other person. As ever, you have to watch out for the ego-mind and its distortions, but if you listen carefully, you can sometimes hear the small, quiet voice of the inner self. And what it usually says (though maybe not in words) is that here is another being, like you, seeking love.

Suddenly you see them in an altogether different light. They seem totally changed. And yet they have done nothing; it is only *you* who has changed.

This is not to suggest that changing our perceptions will resolve all the difficulties we encounter in our relationships. Letting go of our judgments may make another person's behavior comprehensible, but it does not make them right. However, if we can approach such issues from a genuine love rather than from anger and resentment, the chances of our responding in a constructive manner will be much greater. I know that in the case of the colleague who lied to me, once I had defused my anger, I was able to deal with him much more effectively than I would have if I had continued feeling bitter and hostile.

Love in Action

In the preceding chapter, we saw how relationships can easily turn into a vicious circle of mutual attack. It may be very subtle — just a withholding of information, distancing body language, an aloof tone of voice, cynical comments, or personal criticisms. Or it may sometimes be more overt, leading to arguments, fights, or total noncommunication. But whatever form it takes, the underlying game is the same. We are trying to hurt each other in some way.

Every attack is a withholding of love. We know intuitively that the other person wants to feel loved, and that by withholding love we can exercise some power over them and perhaps manipulate them into giving us what we really want. But what we really want is exactly the same as what they really want: We both want to feel loved by others. And we attempt to make others behave in a more loving way toward us by withholding our love from them. Seen from this perspective, the withholding of love is clearly counterproductive and will never work. This is one reason so many couples end up in therapy or in the divorce courts.

This vicious circle can be broken if two people start from the recognition that each wants to feel more loved and more at peace, and then communicate with the conscious intention that the other person will feel loved and at peace, not unloved and hurt. The Buddha called this "right speech": If you cannot say something in such a way that the other person feels good on hearing it, it is better to retain noble silence.

This should not be interpreted as a copout. "Oh, I have something difficult to say, and I don't know how to say it in such a way that you won't feel hurt, so I will just keep quiet." We need to get our feelings out, but we need to do so in a way that does not initiate the vicious circle of mutual attack. So you should retain noble silence only as long as you need to, while you work out how to say what you have to say in a loving manner.

How can we do this? There are several things that can help:

- Become vigilant against attacking thoughts, and filter them out before you speak.

- Put yourself in the other person's shoes. Try to avoid using words or examples that they might construe as attacking, even if no attack is intended.

- When you have something difficult to say, preface it with the reason you want to say it, letting the person know it comes from a place of love rather than one of attack. To say "I love you and really value our relationship, and in order to make it even better for both of us, I need to discuss an issue that is difficult for me" will set a very different tone from that of simply blurting out whatever you have to say. Speaking the truth is one thing; how you say it is quite another.

- Express your fears. They are also part of the truth, and expressing your fear of rejection, being misunderstood, and so on, helps the other person appreciate where you are coming from, and can put the other person more at ease—which, remember, is the goal of this exercise.

- Learn what works. If, despite your best intentions, the other person feels attacked or unloved because of something you said, ask them for suggestions as to how you could have said it better. You will be surprised by how much you can learn.

- When this practice slips, as it surely will from time to time, and the attacking mode creeps in, apologize. Don't let it start up the vicious circle again; instead, acknowledge your mistake (we are all human, after all) and say "I'm sorry, that wasn't fair; there was an element of attack there." Then try to express it with a more loving intention.

When two people in a relationship share the intention of removing any element of attack from their interaction so that they may both feel more loved and more at peace, everything changes. A whole new quality of love appears in the relationship.

In addition to the qualities of *eros*, the passion of love that we know so well, and the quality of *agape*, the Greek word for unconditional love—the compassion that we find when we let go of the judgments we hold against others—there comes the quality of *caritas*, the Latin word for caring, sometimes translated as "charity," as in "faith, hope and charity." *Caritas*, or caring, is not so much an emotion as an attitude. It is love in action. When this is present in a relationship, a miracle unfolds. And it all comes from consciously trying to *give* the experience of peace to the other rather than from trying to withhold it.

All Our Relations

Our intimate relationships may be where we begin the practice of this yoga, but it does not end there. The same principles apply to our relationships with people we hardly know, or may never even have met.

To take just one example, I have never met the political leader of my country. However, I have read much about him in the press, seen him on television, and heard some of the things he has said. As a result, I have formed a great many impressions of him. I have opinions as to ways in which he is right, and ways in which he is wrong. But all of this is my projection. I do not know what goes on inside his mind, how he sees the world, and what he knows that I do not know. I do not know what his personal hopes and fears are, or why he makes the decisions he does. I can only surmise that given his own history, experiences, and conditioning, he is doing the best he knows how.

This does not mean I agree with his actions. If I feel certain policies do not serve people as well as others might, I will do whatever seems most appropriate to try to change the situation. On the other hand, I also try not to let my judgment of his decisions become a judgment of him as a person. I try—and frequently it is not easy—to see him as another fellow being seeking peace.

We can practice the same thing with complete strangers: people we see in the street, on a bus or plane, in a restaurant. We can practice seeing past their actions and appearances, past the judgments we project onto them, and see that invisible part of them that is in so many ways just like us.

Similarly with nonhuman beings: the dogs, dolphins, and dragonflies we meet are also conscious beings. They may not have developed the same mode of consciousness as we have. They have different senses, which give them different experiences of reality; they have different ways of interacting with the world, giving a different color to their consciousness. Dogs hear sounds far beyond the human range, and their sense of smell is a million times more sensitive than ours; dolphins, with their sonar, are aware of altogether different dimensions of experience. Nevertheless, whatever the creature, the essence of consciousness or sentience remains the same: it is the essence of being aware, the light behind all experience. Seeing this, seeing that the consciousness within ourselves is the same consciousness that lies within all sentient beings, is the basis of universal love, a love for all creation.

Meditation –
The Art of Letting Go

In order that the mind should see light instead of darkness, so the entire soul must be turned away from this changing world, until its eye can learn to contemplate reality and that supreme splendor which we have called the good. Hence there may well be an art whose aim would be to effect this very thing.

— Socrates

In addition to our character, our personality, our habits, our beliefs, our hopes, the mistakes we have made, and all the other things that contribute to our sense of being an individual self, there is a dimension of our identity that we cannot describe so easily.

We all know what it means to say "I"—we use the word all the time. Or rather, we think we know what the word means. We can define many of the things we identify ourselves with, but the underlying Self that is doing the identifying is much harder to define. Trying to describe the Self is rather like setting out with a flashlight to search for the source of the flashlight's light. All I would find as I shone the flashlight around would be the various objects that the beam fell upon. However hard I looked I could not locate the source of light. It is the same when I try to discover the nature of "I." All that I am aware of are various aspects of my self that the light of consciousness happens to fall upon—my personality, character, memories, ambitions, habits, beliefs, feelings, intelligence, failings, and so on. Try as I may, I cannot find the source of that light. I cannot find the source of my own experience, the unchanging, permanent core of my being.

Because the essence of I-ness is so hard to describe and define, we identify ourselves with the more tangible aspects—with our physical form, our personality, our profession, our position, our past, our potential, and so on. But such attributes are conditioned by events and can change with time. They do not constitute a single, permanent, unchanging, independent Self.

To become more directly acquainted with the underlying Self has been an eternal quest of humanity. It was this call that was inscribed above the portals of the ancient Greek oracle at Delphi, Gnothi Seauton—"Know Thyself." And in one way or another it is the core of most of the major world religions.

A Still Mind

A common aim of many techniques of meditation is to bring mental activity to an end and so reach what Indian teachings describe as samadhi—a state of "still mind." A still mind is a mind that is free from fear, free from fantasies, free from ruminations about the past, free from concern about what may or may not be happening to it. It is a mind no longer disturbed by the many thoughts that come from believing that fulfillment lies in what we have or what we do. For once, the ego-mind has fallen silent.

Consciousness itself remains; you are still awake, you are still aware. You, the experiencer, still exist. For a while, you are free from your hopes and fears, your social status, your character and personality, and all the other things that gave you a sense of personal identity. You are free to know the underlying Self.

Such knowing comes not as an idea or an understanding, for that would make the subject of experience an object of experience. Besides, the still mind is a mind that is not moved by ideas or understandings—at least, not as we normally think of them. This knowing comes from a direct acquaintance with the Self. I simply AM. I am not any thing; there is no substance or form to my being. Yet its reality is absolutely clear—and undeniable.

It is this transcendence of the ego and remembering of one's underlying nature that give meditation its value. Here are the identity, peace, and serenity that we have been searching for all along. Here is the fulfillment for which we have been yearning. Then, when we come out of meditation, we return to active life with a taste of this inner truth, feeling a little less attached to the things of the world.

No single moment of transcendence is likely to enlighten us forever. Our conditioning is so deep that it is not long before we once again are caught up in our hopes, fears, worries, and concerns, and once again start looking for external sources of fulfillment. But a little of the taste remains, and our attachment to the world may not be quite as strong as it was before . . . and perhaps after another taste, a little less strong still. This is why regular meditation practice is usually recommended: a daily dose of dehypnosis, a daily remembering of ourselves in our unconditioned state.

Different, Not Difficult

Meditation is often thought of as an *activity* of the mind, some form of mental "doing." However, a mental activity does not easily lead to a state of stillness, and meditative practices that take this approach tend to be very difficult. True meditation is not difficult so much as different—completely different from the mental processes we are accustomed to.

Most techniques aimed at stilling the mind are exercises in attention rather than exercises in thinking. One does not quiet the mind by changing what one thinks, but by changing the direction and quality of one's attention. In their own particular ways, meditation techniques shift the attention away from the world of the senses—the world we once thought would bring us peace of mind—and turn the attention inward, toward our inner essence.

As the mind begins to settle down, it discovers an inner calm and peace. The attention has found what it has been seeking all along, and needs no coercion to continue in this direction. This is reflected in the following lines by Maharishi Mahesh Yogi, the teacher of Transcendental Meditation, taken from his book *The Science of Being and Art of Living*:

> To go to a field of greater happiness is the natural tendency of the mind. Because in the practice of transcendental meditation the conscious mind is set on the way to experiencing bliss-consciousness, the mind finds the way increasingly attractive as it advances in the direction of bliss. It finds increasing charm at every step of its march. This practice is, therefore, not only simple but also automatic.

Practice

In this respect, the art of meditation can be the essence of easiness. It is just letting go—allowing the mind to return to its natural state of its own accord.

Any difficulty that may be experienced usually comes from the difficulty involved in unhooking the mind from its conditioned thinking. So strong is our attachment to finding happiness through the world we experience—and this includes not just what we experience through our eyes, ears, and skin, but also the things we see, hear, and feel in our imagination—that the mind holds on tightly to its cherished beliefs.

Even when we do let go and the mind begins to relax and settle down, it is usually not long before it is disturbed again as some unfulfilled desire starts once more to work out ways of finding future satisfaction. In this respect, ironically, stilling the mind is not at all easy.

This is why specific techniques of meditation are of value, not as things to do, but as aids to release the mind from its deeply ingrained patterns. They are skills we can learn to disengage our egoic mode of thinking.

Divine Union

Another important consequence of allowing the mind to sink into the silence of pure consciousness is that the qualities that usually distinguish one self from another are no longer there. All markers of individuality have gone. We become aware that we are the light of consciousness, and that this light is the same light that shines within all beings. We become one with all beings.

This is the divine union of which so many great saints and mystics have spoken. And, as they have repeatedly told us, it is only through a direct personal knowing of our deep inner unity with all beings that we will be saved.

This is our challenge. Can we wake up in time? Can we continue our evolutionary journey and grow from our current state of semi-wakefulness into the full realization of our true identity? This may sound like a lofty goal, but it is, in fact, where each of our lives is taking us. It is just the state of full human maturity.

Maturity –
Coming of Age

The distance between man and the gods is not all that much greater than the distance between beasts and man. We have already closed the latter gap, and there is no reason to suppose that we shall not eventually close the former.

—Ken Wilber

Our state of semiawakening is not something we are stuck with. It is just a reflection of our as-yet-incomplete inner development, both as individuals and as a species.

It has long been recognized that from the moment of conception, our biological development mirrors the evolution of our species. Like the first life on Earth, our own life starts as a single cell. This cell divides, becoming a simple colony, and folds in upon itself to form a

119

simple tube, much as early multicellular organisms started off as simple "feeding tubes." After a few weeks, the growing embryo develops gills as if it were becoming a fish. Then it resembles a reptile, and a little later takes on some of the characteristics of smaller mammals. Even at week ten, it still has a tail.

Scientists sum up these parallels in the phrase "Ontogeny recapitulates phylogeny." In simpler English, that means, "The development of the individual (ontogeny) repeats the pattern of the development of the species (phylogeny)."

Although the principle is usually applied only to our biological development, a similar pattern can be seen in our psychological development. The stages that our species went through in the evolution of its consciousness are paralleled in the newborn human being as it embarks on its own journey of inner development.

A year or so into life, we start to walk—something our hominid ancestors first did several million years ago. During our second year, we learn to use words; and later we begin to entertain ideas and make abstractions—developments that parallel the evolution of language and thought since the emergence of homo erectus.

As we grow, so does our awareness. To begin with, we are learning how to interpret the data pouring in through our senses and how to control our bodies. At this stage, there is little distinction between self and surroundings. A sense of individuality begins to dawn only as we move from total dependence on our mothers toward greater autonomy. We learn how to use our hands and how to create change in the world. We discover relationships of cause and effect, and develop a will. Through this growing interaction with the world comes the realization that we are independent entities, people in our own right. As our facility with language develops, we begin to give expression to this realization. "I like this." "I want that." "I can do this."

These steps in inner development would seem to mirror the stages that early humanity passed through. To begin with, the general consciousness was probably similar to that of a young child—primitive humans were aware of the world and aware of themselves as physical beings, but had little sense of an individual self. If there was any sense of identity, it was of oneness with the Great Mother—Nature, the provider of all.

It was the development of tools and the move away from an agrarian culture toward urban civilization that sowed the seeds for the emergence of a more egoic consciousness. We discovered our ability to change the world, to influence the behavior of the Great Mother. A new sense of identity had been born. We were something special — separate, independent beings with a will of our own.

The Wisdom of the Young

Let us return to the image of the child. One almost universal characteristic of young children is their purity. What mother has not looked at her young child and marveled at the light that shines through him? Children have an innocence that adults have lost, an awareness of simple truths that we have forgotten. They are reminders of the way we too once were.

This purity seems to be something innate. Children do not learn it from their parents; on the contrary, parents frequently find their children to be their teachers in these matters. Nor is it something they are educated into; if anything, they are educated out of it. More likely, it is a reflection of human consciousness in its natural, unsullied state.

It is the same with the development of our species. What evidence we have of life in early communities suggests a much greater respect for nature, and attitudes less materialistic than those found in modern civilization. Some of the evidence for this is archaeological, but we can also get a good idea of how our ancestors may have lived by looking at various contemporary indigenous cultures that have not yet been overly influenced by contact with Western civilization: the Kogi of Colombia, the Bushmen of the Kalahari, the Penan in Malaysia. These people often know many simple truths that we appear to have forgotten. They smile at our attachment to things, and at the energy we put into trying to be masters of our world. In general, they are content with life. They have a deep respect for their local ecology, and for knowledge of how to live in harmony with the land and with other living beings. Moreover, like little children, they can be teachers to us, reminding us of the innocence we have lost in the rush of progress — and of the wisdom that we are now seeking to regain.

The Descent into Matter

The loss of purity, both in the growing child and in a technological society, is probably unavoidable. It is part of the process of development, part of our engagement with the world of matter. The more a child learns how to control the world, the more fascinated he becomes with his discoveries—with what he can do and with what he can achieve.

Likewise with our social development. As our tools became more powerful and our understanding of the world deepened, we became fascinated by the changes we could create. Our urge to improve the quality of life led to the Industrial Revolution. And its successes reinforced our infatuation with the material world.

The more ways we discovered to manipulate and change the world, the more our belief that we were individuals, in control of our own destinies, was strengthened. As our abilities grew, we seduced ourselves into believing that such prowess could satisfy *all* our needs, psychological as well as physical.

This preoccupation with our own well-being led us to become increasingly self-centered. More and more, we saw ourselves as separate individuals, each concerned with his or her own fulfillment, competing with others for the means to achieve it—with all the dangers that entails. Less and less were we prepared to devote ourselves to the group; indeed, the more industrialized we became, the more self-interest became a virtue.

This sense of separateness was further boosted by a scientific paradigm that saw the world as a mechanism, devoid of spirit. Like a boisterous teenager, we became full of ourselves and our capacities, relishing our newfound sense of freedom from the family. But in this case, the "family" that had brought us up and supported us so far, and from which we were now separating ourselves, was Mother Earth.

Ontogeny Heralds Phylogeny

Important as it is to see our absorption with material things as an unavoidable phase in our development, it is equally important to see it as a passing phase. Most of us do move beyond adolescence. We learn from our experience (to varying degrees). We learn to be less self-centered; we learn to take responsibility for our actions.

As we grow older, we admit that there is much we do not know and will never know. We become wiser about human nature—its virtues and its failings. We accept the ways of nature. We become less attached to our possessions; less upset by events of little consequence; less needful of others' appreciation. Many of us become better at living in the present. And some of us come to accept our own mortality.

A few of us may even come to know that we are free, that our well-being is not dependent on the world we perceive. These enlightened ones may release themselves from all their imagined burdens and find true peace of mind. They may even complete their inner awakening and come to know the nature of consciousness as fully as we now know the world of form. These are the ones we call the saints and mystics—those whose lives have illuminated the history of humanity: the awakened ones.

At the moment, full maturity is still a rarity. But rather than considering such individuals to be exceptions, we should think of them as heralds. They are portents of what could lie ahead of us as our own inner maturity blossoms. They are also portents of what could lie ahead for the human race if we survive our troubled adolescence.

In this respect, ontogeny *heralds* phylogeny. Both as individuals and as a species, we are heading in the direction of self-liberation.

Freedom –
Emancipation from Matter

These things shall be—a loftier race
Than e'er the world hath known shall rise
With flame of freedom in their souls,
And light of knowledge in their eyes.

—John Symonds

Both human development and the evolution of life share another significant trend: a journey toward greater freedom from physical constraints.

Some early evolutionary examples of increasing degrees of freedom are the processes by which living systems obtained energy. Biologists believe that early living cells used simple fermentation. These bacteria broke down sugar molecules into smaller molecules such as carbon dioxide and water, taking for their own use the energy that had bound these molecules together.

This process was limited by the availability of these sugars and of certain acids, and after a while (a billion years or so) supplies began to run low. Some bacteria escaped from this constraint by developing a new way of obtaining food: photosynthesis. Using the energy of sunlight, they converted carbon dioxide, water, and minerals into energy-rich organic compounds. Since these simpler molecules were much more abundant than the sugars needed for fermentation, the new cells could survive in a greater variety of environments. A new degree of freedom had been reached.

But this process had its own drawbacks: It produced oxygen as a waste product. To us, oxygen might seem a most beneficial gas, yet it is a very reactive chemical. Combining readily with many other substances, it can destroy many of the complex molecules on which life depends. To the cells of the time, it was poisonous pollution.

After several hundred million years, so much oxygen had accumulated in the atmosphere that it threatened life on Earth. Nature's response was to exploit oxygen's destructive qualities and capture the energy released as oxygen reduced larger molecules into smaller components. This new process of obtaining energy—called respiration—was far more efficient than either fermentation or photosynthesis, and greatly expanded the range of resources at life's disposal. With respiration, organisms were not limited to sugars and minerals for food; they could extract energy from the more complex molecules that fermentation and photosynthesis created. Life could now feed on the products of other living systems. A major new branch of evolution had emerged: the animal kingdom.

The animals that first colonized the land were amphibians. But they could never roam far from water. Even toads, which spend most of their life on land, have to return to water in order to reproduce, since tadpoles (their larval stage) must live in water. Reptiles overcame this hurdle by developing tough shells for their eggs, encapsulating a watery environment for the growing embryo. Their eggs could be laid on dry land, miles from any water—another degree of freedom.

Another step toward greater freedom was warm blood. Since heat speeds up chemical reactions, the rate at which an organism can convert food into energy is a function of its temperature. Cold-blooded animals such as snakes and lizards rely largely on the sun for warmth, absorbing its heat directly into their bodies. When there is no sun to bask in, these creatures become quite sluggish. Warm-blooded animals—namely, birds and mammals—have overcome this handicap by developing an internal heating system that keeps the whole body at the optimum temperature for its metabolism. Being less dependent on the temperature of their surroundings has given them a new degree of freedom. They can be active under a wide variety of conditions and can inhabit regions too cold for reptiles.

The Freeing of Humanity

With human beings came many new degrees of freedom. Speech freed us from the limitation of learning only from our individual experience. Our ability to deliberate on the future gave us a certain freedom of will; we could choose those actions that offer us better chances of survival, or those that enhance our comfort and well-being.

Walking on two legs, rather than four, meant that our hands were free to do many new and useful things. Now we did not have to chase our prey; we could set traps for it. Being able to create clothes and shelter freed us to live in cooler climates. The wheel further enhanced our freedom of movement, giving us the means to transport heavy loads with much less effort. Agriculture brought us other liberties, enabling us to raise our own animals, grow our own crops, and store our harvests for later use.

As we settled in communities, individuals took on differing responsibilities. Some caught the food; others prepared it. Some made the clothes; some collected water; others built new shelters. This increasing specialization brought greater efficiency, and with it yet greater emancipation from the constraints of the physical world. We were free to take on other activities such as pottery, smelting, forging, tanning, spinning, weaving, carving, healing, teaching, writing, painting, sculpting, and music-making.

Yet more liberation came with the Industrial Revolution. No longer did we have to spend most of our life tilling the land; we were free to improve the quality of life in many ways. The steam engine freed us from dependence on sheer muscle power. Machinery of all kinds increased the efficiency of production, resulting in a plethora of material goods that allowed us to perform more tasks and achieve grander goals. Sturdier ships, railways, and later automobiles and planes gave us far greater freedom of movement and allowed industry to use resources from all over the globe. Medical discoveries relieved us from the scourge of many diseases, freed us from much physical pain, and helped us recover from physical injury. In these and other ways, the Industrial Revolution liberated us from many of the constraints of our bodies and from many of the limits imposed by our environment.

Today, information technology is leading to an emancipation from work itself. Automated factories produce cars, electric motors, television sets, radios, cameras, computers, and digital watches with almost no input of human energy. In banks, offices, warehouses, and supermarkets, information technology is increasingly taking over functions previously performed by people. Accountants, lawyers, pilots, architects, draftsmen, doctors, engineers, secretaries, and others are being released from many of their routine tasks.

The consequence is plain to see. The more developed nations are no longer heading toward full employment but toward ever-increasing unemployment. Unemployment is usually seen as undesirable, both personally and socially, and something to be fought against at all costs. Yet, somewhat ironically, it is the very thing we have been striving for.

From the dawn of civilization, people have been seeking to work less—not more. To this end we have invented a wealth of labor-saving equipment—plows, windmills, waterwheels, pumps, weaving looms, milking machines, combine harvesters, elevators, washing machines, food processors, microwave ovens, power drills, vacuum cleaners, automatic car washes, and motorized golf carts, to name just a few. The intention behind almost every technological development, from the first stone axe to the automated teller machine, has been to reduce the time and energy we spend in physical toil. Yet now that we are finally seeing the fruits of our labor-saving efforts, we are holding on fiercely to the very thing we have tried for so long to leave behind.

On the one hand we love work for what it brings—security, self-esteem, comforts, human contact, challenge. On the other hand we resent it for what it demands of us—the time we have to spend at it, the energy and freedom it seems to take from us. How many of us, if given the money we now receive from work, would still choose to spend our time in an office, a truck, a store, a print shop, or a coal mine? The majority want what work gives, not the work itself.

We fear unemployment not because we fear the loss of work itself, but because we fear financial insecurity, uncertainty, loss of self-esteem, material discomfort, and possibly hunger—all things that work has helped us avoid. In addition, since our economies are based on the input of human labor (human time is the principal component of any price, the natural resources being intrinsically free), wide-scale unemployment can spell disaster for a nation's economic well-being.

The question we should be asking is not how to maintain employment, but how to create an economic system that can distribute resources and enhance our well-being, while at the same time fulfilling our age-old wish to be free from unwanted toil.

Freedom for What?

Freedom from toil is not the only freedom we have sought. We have fought to be free from oppression, fought to overthrow dictators and tyrants, fought for the freedom to vote for the government of our choice. Nations have battled to gain independence from other nations, erected statues to proclaim their liberty, and stamped declarations of that liberty on their money. We have struggled for freedom from slavery, freedom from prejudice, and freedom from persecution; for the freedom to say what we believe, to live where we wish, and to worship as we choose.

But what is all this freedom for?

Our underlying motivation, as ever, is to move away from pain and suffering toward greater joy and contentment. This is the underlying freedom for which we have worked and fought: to be free from all that seems to stop us from finding peace and fulfillment.

To an extent, we have been successful. We have eliminated or reduced many sources of suffering. We have found ways to satisfy most of the body's needs. We have increased our standard of living. We have been able to fulfill many of our desires. But are we really any happier?

In 1955, a study was conducted to find out how many people in America were happy with what they had in life. At that time, 30% of those polled felt they were happy with their lot. The same study was repeated in 1992. Over the intervening 37 years, the material standard of living had improved considerably: Per capita income and consumption had both doubled, average house size had doubled, the number of cars per family had nearly tripled, the number of TV stations had increased by a factor of twenty or more (and the picture had gone from black-and-white to color). Yet the number of people who were happy with their lot was exactly the same: 30%.

Two conclusions can be drawn from this. First, material well-being is not equivalent to inner well-being. Second, the percentage of the population who know how to be happy has not changed at all. We have done almost nothing to educate people in one of the basic wisdoms of life. In this respect, we are still far from free.

The Freedom to Be Free

A mind that is caught up in the past is not free—no more free than a mind caught up in concerns about what may or may not happen in the future. A person worried about the opinions of others or anxious for security is not really free. We are not free if imagined fears drive our perceptions and our decisions. Nor is our thinking free if we judge someone on the basis of their race, dress, profession, accent, or beliefs.

We saw earlier that we already possess most of the understanding and technology necessary to avert environmental catastrophe. And we have the money. What we do not have is the will to do what we know is needed. Free will requires a free mind, not one caught up in worry and concern.

To be truly free, we need to move beyond our cultural conditioning. We need to release ourselves from our attachments, from our concern for past and future times. We need to be free of our illusions; free from unnecessary fear.

The freedom we now need is the inner freedom that allows us to think more intelligently. The freedom to draw more deeply on our creativity and use it in ways that are in our true best interests; the freedom to follow our vision and find that which we truly seek.

This is the opportunity that our many physical freedoms are opening us to: self-liberation. The freeing of our minds so that we may be our true, authentic selves.

This new freedom requires a new kind of work—work on ourselves. In this respect, we have not reached the end of work at all. There has merely been a shift in the arena of work from outer to inner—a shift to the next phase in human evolution.

The Future

The human heart can go to the lengths of God.
Dark and cold we may be, but this
Is no winter now. The frozen misery
Of centuries breaks, cracks, begins to move;
The thunder is the thunder of the floes,
The thaw, the flood, the upstart Spring.
Thank God our time is now when wrong
Comes up to face us everywhere,
Never to leave us 'til we take
The longest stride of soul men ever took.
Affairs are now soul size.
The enterprise is exploration into God.
Where are you making for? It takes
So many thousand years to wake,
But will you wake for pity's sake?

—Christopher Fry, A *Sleep of Prisoners*

Challenge –
Crisis as Opportunity

When a seed—or an animal—or a man is ripe, it must mature to its next phase. Or rot.

—Stewart Edward White

In the second part of this book, we saw how the various environmental, economic, and social problems confronting us are symptomatic of a deeper underlying crisis in our thinking, perception, and values.

This crisis has been coming for a long time. Its seeds were sown some fifty thousand years ago, when *Homo sapiens*, the creature with an enlarged neocortex, began to use its complex brain in new ways. Something different was walking on the earth: a species whose future

135

was determined not by its genes so much as by its ideas. A species that could begin to understand the Universe in which it found itself. A species with unprecedented creativity. So new were these developments that some anthropologists gave this species a new name, *Homo sapiens sapiens*, the "wise human being."

Quite naturally, we turned our new capacities to the creation of a better world for ourselves. A world in which food was plentiful and available all year round. A world in which we could protect ourselves from cold and rain. A world in which disease did not strike us so young or so often. A world in which we could live longer and more fulfilling lives.

We set out with the best of intentions: to reduce suffering and be more at peace. But unwittingly we fell into the trap of assuming that the inner needs we were now experiencing could be met in the same way as our physical needs—through having or doing the right things. Not realizing that true peace could be found within ourselves, we were seduced by the material world and all its fruits.

The consequences of this error were benign at first. Only later, as our tools grew more powerful, did problems appear. For not only did technology amplify our ability to satisfy our physical needs; it also amplified our ability to satisfy our psychological needs. The burden we placed on the physical world rapidly increased, and suddenly we found ourselves a threat to millions of species, including our own.

Seeing the writing on the wall, we have begun awakening to our responsibilities, both for what we have done and for what we should do. But now, at the very time we most need to change, we find ourselves unable to let go. We cling to our many comforts, apparently unwilling to bear the modest *dis*comforts that would enhance our chances of survival. Too many people seem to prefer risking annihilation to giving up their beliefs and attachments.

So we stand by, watching the living Earth erode, and wonder how humanity could continue to be so crazy.

The crisis that has been brewing for millennia is upon us.

Crises as Drivers

Crises are generally seen as undesirable; they imply danger and potential misfortune. There are good reasons for this. A crisis is a sign that the old ways are no longer working and something new is called for. In such times, there can be very real danger: if appropriate responses are not made rapidly, the old order may begin to collapse.

This is all too possible with humanity today. If we do not address the deeper spiritual issues underlying the many problems we face, it is very likely that civilization will fall apart.

On the other hand, any crisis, big or small, personal or planetary, also presents an opportunity—something the ancient Chinese seemed well aware of. Their word for crisis, *wei-chi*, is written as a combination of two characters, one meaning "danger," the other "opportunity." The opportunity may not always be easy to see, but it is always there. It is the chance to remedy what is wrong and move on to a new way of being.

In this respect, crises are a challenge—the challenge to recognize what is no longer working and seize the opportunity to learn, make changes, and progress. Thus, crises can play a crucial role in evolution.

Evolutionary Crises

In the previous chapter, we considered the early planetary crisis that occurred as simple bacteria began running short of food—the first of many food crises. The response to this crisis was a new way of obtaining energy: photosynthesis.

Over the next one-and-one-half billion years, oxygen, the "poisonous" by-product of photosynthesis, accumulated in the atmosphere until eventually it threatened to extinguish life on Earth. Life responded to this crisis with a new type of organism, one that could feed on oxygen.

Later, as cells grew larger, they faced a different sort of food crisis. If a cell's diameter doubled, its surface area quadrupled and its volume increased eightfold. To keep this larger volume fed, the cell's walls had to absorb nutrients twice as fast. The larger cells grew, the more difficult it became for them to feed themselves—another crisis, another danger, and another sign that something new was called for. The response this time was the multicellular organism: cells stayed the same size, but the organism of which they were part was free to grow.

Today, life on Earth has arrived at another crisis. The values that have guided the human species through most of its development are no longer working. Preservation of the self may have been very valuable in prehistoric times. It may also have been valuable when the world was a collection of independent communities and states—although, even then, self-centeredness among those in power often led to greed, exploitation, and corruption. But today such values have become extremely dangerous. Directing powerful technologies with a global reach, they spell disaster.

Once again, the old way—in this case, our mode of consciousness—is no longer working. Once again, a new way is called for.

The Opportunity

This is the real opportunity nestling within our global crisis: the opportunity to develop a new mode of consciousness—a new way of seeing and a new way of thinking. This could be the next evolutionary adaptation waiting to emerge. Not, as we have seen, a biological adaptation; there is no time for that, and even if we could genetically re-engineer ourselves, it would not hit at the heart of the problem. What the crisis is driving us toward is inner change, a transformation into truly wise human beings, no longer fettered by self-centeredness.

It is driving us toward a new perception of ourselves, a new sense of purpose, a new way of being.

Apocalypse —
Premonitions of Transformation

The world, as we know it, is coming to an end. The world as the center of the Universe, the world divided from the heavens, the world bound by horizons in which love is reserved for the members of the in group: that is the world that is passing away. Apocalypse does not point to a fiery Armageddon but to the fact that our ignorance and our complacency are coming to an end.

—Joseph Campbell

The various manifestations of our crisis have not yet forced us to explore their underlying cause. When there is a disaster—an oil spill, a bank crash, a nuclear accident, a crop failure, or an industrial tragedy—we still treat it as an isolated event. We regret that it occurred and do our best to clear up the mess. Not recognizing the inner malaise that lies at the root of these disasters, we continue treating only the symptoms of the problem. We are like a doctor who lances a boil on a patient's skin without stopping to consider what is causing it.

These symptoms will not suddenly go away. They will continue to become more severe. We are reaping the consequences of many years of misguided thinking, of decisions made through self-centered and materialist value systems. Moreover, as we continue along our mistaken path, we will probably find ourselves facing economic, environmental, and social catastrophes that make Chernobyl, Bhopal, the Exxon Valdez, and even Katrina seem tame. As the refrain goes, "You ain't seen nothin' yet!"

Perhaps we need these growing catastrophes. The disasters we have experienced to date have not alerted us to the underlying errors in our minds, at least not enough of us to make much difference. Louder alarm bells will be necessary if we are to awaken from our slumbers. Indeed, our culture may have to be shaken at its roots before we come to our senses.

Millennial Fever

Prophecies of disaster are not new. Throughout history, there have been dire warnings of the tragedies that would befall humanity, and even of the end of the world.

Various dates have been proposed for these ultimate catastrophes. Many thought the turn of the first millennium, A.D. 1000, would be the end. The twelfth-century Cistercian abbot, Joachim of Fiore, thought the end would come in the year 1200. Hardly a century has turned without large numbers of people prophesying that the end was nigh. Thus, at the recent turn of the new millennium, it was not surprising to find many contemporary apocalyptical prophecies focusing on the year 2000.

Why, then, should we take current warnings any more seriously than previous ones? All earlier forecasts of doom have failed to materialize; what reason is there to suppose that current ones will be any different?

No reason. Except that this is the time when the global environmental crisis has come upon us. Never before in human history have the dangers been so acute, nor the likelihood of catastrophe so real.

Never before has the very survival of the planet's biosystem been at stake. Danger seems to be coming from all sides at once. Suddenly there is very good reason to wonder whether we will make it very far into the current millennium.

If ever there was a justification for millennial fever, it is before us now.

Apocalypse Now?

Many historical prophecies herald events that do bear a remarkable resemblance to the times we are passing through and the dangers we face. Take, for example, the centuries-old prophecy of the North American Hopi Indians. They foresaw the coming of the white man from the East; his invention of carriages that need no horses; and his ability to travel along roads in the sky. One part of the Hopi prophecy seems to predict World War II; another matches well with the establishment of the United Nations; others detail the death and destruction that the white man would bring, and his desecration of the land. There are also possible allusions to nuclear weapons: "a gourd of ashes" that would fall from the sky, boiling the oceans and burning the land so that nothing would grow for many years. This would be the signal that the final stage was approaching. Man would travel to the moon and build a city in the sky, but then go no farther.

However, the Hopi prophecy also says that at the height of the white man's foolishness great wisdom returns, coming from the East. If he listens to this wisdom, there will come a conscious transformation and rebirth of humanity; if not, there will follow the ending of all life. This last part is particularly worth noting. It does not foretell a fixed future, but a future in which we have choice—and that choice involves a spiritual awakening.

This notion that wisdom will come from the East is also found in Tibetan Buddhism. In the eighth century, Padma Sambhava prophesied that "when the iron bird flies in the sky and the horses run on wheels, the Dharma [the teaching] will move to the West."

The Judeo-Christian tradition contains several similar predictions. The Old Testament books of Samuel, Elijah, Amos, Jeremiah, Ezekiel, Habakkah, Isaiah, and Joel all foretell troubled times to come. The latter two, for example, both speak of the coming "Day of the Lord," when the land is laid desolate and the sky so darkened that neither moon nor sun can be seen. Could this be a description of a nuclear holocaust, or some environmental catastrophe?

In the New Testament, we find Jesus on the Mount of Olives, fore-telling a time when there would be many wars, famines, pestilence, and earthquakes. Such events would be the sign that this age was coming to a close. Of course, it is impossible to say whether he was referring to events two thousand years ahead or to some other time, but his descriptions are certainly relevant. The actual frequency of earthquakes may not have increased in recent times, but their impact on densely populated urban areas is much greater. So too is the impact of war: napalm, land mines, anthrax, and nuclear weapons inflict far more damage on communities and on the environment than did bows and arrows and spears. Famines hit with increasing severity, exacerbated by the population explosion and the depletion of the soil. And the possibility of new pestilences strikes fear deep into the hearts of individuals and insurance companies alike.

These correlations are often seen as a sign that the "Day of Judgment" is indeed nigh. But we should also remember that when Jesus warned of future tribulations, and of religious persecution, false prophets, and impostors claiming to be the risen Christ, he was speaking not of the end of the world, but of "the pains of birth." There would, he declared, be light on the other side.

The Revelation of St. John

These prophecies bear a close resemblance to the Apocalypse (the word means "Revelation") of St. John. In this final book of the New Testament, John gives a detailed account of his vision and of the events that would herald the final day of judgment. He tells of a scroll with seven seals representing the retributions that must come. The first four release the famous horsemen bringing war, famine, disease, and death. He saw seven angels with seven trumpets, each foretelling disaster. Seven bowls are poured out: ugly and painful sores, lifeless seas, the shedding of blood, scorching by the sun, darkness, deserts, and an earthquake like none known before. Again, it is easy to see how these predictions appear to be coming true today.

Then comes the appearance of the Antichrist. He, says St. John, is the secular savior, who offers the hope of peace by claiming to be able to resolve the problems of the world. Not recognizing him for what he is, people rally to his call and his influence spreads into all nations.

The Antichrist's promises are, however, empty. Wars continue to proliferate, taking humanity to the brink of annihilation. Then in the final conflict, the battle of Armageddon, Christ returns and the Antichrist is finally defeated. Christ's kingdom reigns and the gospel spreads across the earth.

Revisioning Armageddon

Most spiritual scriptures have several levels of interpretation. There is the surface meaning, the literal everyday level of interpretation; and there are other, deeper layers of meaning, and spiritual metaphors. The revelations of St. John regarding the Antichrist are no exception.

As we've seen, we are all to some extent hypnotized by our prevailing culture into believing that our salvation lies in the material world, and in what we have or do. It is this that underlies much of our egocentricity and many of our malignant behavior patterns. Yet we've also seen that there remains an unhypnotized aspect of our selves, which knows that inner fulfillment does not depend on the world of the senses. This is our inner guide, waiting quietly to help us when we turn to it. It does not judge; it knows the real nature of unconditional love. It is the part of us that is fully in the present and at perfect peace.

If the Revelation of St. John were to be considered metaphorically as well as literally, Christ would symbolize this inner source of wisdom. The dependent and conditioned mode of thought—the ego-mind—would then be symbolized by the Antichrist. This is the aspect of ourselves that stands against our inner knowing. It is anti—that is, opposed to—the Christ within.

This mode of thinking prevents us from hearing that our inner well-being is not at the mercy of the world around us. Its role is to keep us bound to the material world and to all the many things and experiences that we believe will bring fulfillment. It is the part of us that judges other people in terms of good or bad, friend or foe; that blames others for our own distress; that fears the world may not give us what we want. It is the ego-mind that is caught up in the past and the future.

This error in our own minds is the "secular savior" that would have us believe that by looking to the material world we will find the perfect peace we seek. This false prophet cannot let us see that it is itself the error we must correct. Instead, the ego-mind claims *it* is our true self and the supreme judge of what is right and wrong. This is "Satan in disguise," the prophet of material salvation that lives within us all. And its influence has indeed spread into all nations and into all our affairs.

Yet the promises of this secular savior are empty, just as in St. John's revelation. However much wealth and worldly success we gather, true peace of mind remains as elusive as ever. Meanwhile, our consumption grows exponentially, along with ever-increasing pollution and environmental degradation, taking humanity to the brink of annihilation.

But now, as the writing on the wall accumulates, we are beginning to awaken to the real nature of the conflict we are fighting, the final battle each of us must fight. It is the inner Armageddon, the battle between our ego-mind and our higher self. It is the conflict that each of us is fighting every day—the battle between judgment and letting go, between fear and love, between our cultural conditioning and our inner truth.

As the saying goes, "We have met the enemy and the enemy is us." It is within every one of us. And so is the wisdom that can see us through. We are not facing each other on different sides of the battle. We are each on both sides, all facing ourselves.

The good news is that St. John foresees that the battle of Armageddon will be won by Christ, suggesting that our higher knowing will eventually defeat the Antichrist within. Only then does Christ's kingdom reign. This we could interpret as a world freed from the dictates of our ego-mind, a world in which a liberated mind is the norm rather than the exception, a world in which love, not fear, is the prevailing emotion.

There will, at last, be peace on Earth: the inner peace we have been seeking all along.

Setbacks –
Constructive Extinctions

> . . . but as when
> The bird of wonder dies, the maiden phoenix,
> Her ashes new-create another heir
> As great in admiration as herself.
>
> —William Shakespeare

The possibility that humanity may not pass the test facing it cannot be overlooked. The pathways to failure are both numerous and diverse. We are facing a great range of environmental dangers, and there are probably many more of which we are still unaware. The stress of ever-increasing change could also have disastrous consequences; remember, eighty percent of "accidents" are said to be

145

caused by human error. Nor can we ignore the dangers of war. As resources become less plentiful and social tensions increase, wars of one kind or another become ever more likely, and the weaponry now at our disposal can destroy ecosystems as easily as people.

Any catastrophe, "natural" or otherwise, that destroyed the infrastructure of contemporary civilization could send humanity into a new Dark Age. Serious as that may seem to us, it would be a relatively minor setback for the rest of life.

The consequences would be much more serious if, for instance, the greenhouse effect were to become a runaway effect. It would not be just coastal cities and farmlands that were ruined; the regional ecologies critical to the survival of millions of species would be destroyed. This could result in evolution's being set back millions of years.

The Demise of the Dinosaur

Such setbacks are not new to evolution. A major disaster occurred 66 million years ago, when the dinosaurs' reign came to an abrupt end. And it was not just the dinosaurs that died; millions of other species, both plant and animal, suddenly became extinct.

Exactly what caused this catastrophe is still not certain. That it was some form of environmental disruption is pretty clear. The sedimentary rock that forms the boundary between the time of the dinosaurs, the Cretaceous Era, and the Tertian Era that followed consists of a thin layer of clay. Samples of this clay taken around the world show between a hundred and ten thousand times the normal level of soot. This suggests a colossal, planetwide fire, during which a major proportion of the planet's forests went up in smoke. Supporting evidence comes from the unusual abundance of nitrogen isotopes in this layer; these could have come from heavy acid rain. Another consequence of a planetwide fire would have been a sudden increase in carbon dioxide, perhaps triggering a greenhouse effect.

Clues as to how such a fire may have started can be found in the high levels of iridium in this clay. Iridium is a rare element on Earth but is not so rare in meteors. This, along with the discovery that mineral grains in this layer show signs of intense shock, suggests that a large meteor, perhaps several miles in diameter, struck the earth— and there is strong evidence that a very large impact occurred around that time, 66 million years ago, in the Yucatan Peninsula in Mexico.

As well as starting widespread fires, such an impact would have produced massive clouds of dust. The result could have been very similar to a "nuclear winter." Many plants would have been eliminated, destroying important elements in the food chain—at the top of which were the dinosaurs.

Other researchers have proposed that volcanoes were the cause. Volcanic dust contains high levels of iridium and produces similar layers of clay. And there is geological evidence of an intense period of volcanic activity at about that time, which could well have thrown huge plumes of fiery ash and gases into the upper atmosphere.

It is very possible that both these hypotheses are correct. The impact of a very large meteor could have smashed a hole through the earth's crust, triggering a series of massive volcanic eruptions.

Or perhaps some other series of events was to blame. During the million or so years immediately preceding the dinosaurs' demise, the climate seems to have undergone a series of significant changes. Possibly some phenomenon that we do not yet know about was the trigger—remember that only fifty years ago we knew nothing of the greenhouse effect. All that is certain is that 75 percent, or more, of the earth's species suddenly disappeared.

Past Extinctions

The end of the Cretaceous Era was but one of a series of mass extinctions. Scientists believe there have been at least seven other occasions when the number of species fell suddenly and dramatically. Two hundred and thirteen million years ago, the Triassic Era came to an abrupt end, again with signs of intense shock. (At about the same time, a large meteor created the forty-mile Manicouagan crater in Quebec.)

Two hundred and forty-eight million years ago, another mass extinction resulted in the loss of 90 percent of all species then living, ending the Permian Era of Earth's history.

A hundred million years before that, the Devonian Era ended in a mass extinction of marine life. (Again, the sedimentary rock from around that time shows an unusually high level of iridium.)

About 440 million years ago, three close periods of extinction, associated with major glaciation and lowering of the sea level, brought an end to the Ordovician Era. Other major extinctions are thought to have occurred 500, 570, and 630 million years ago. There may well have been others of which scientists are as yet unaware.

Mass Extinction Now

Today we are experiencing the start of another mass extinction. This time, however, it is not meteors or volcanoes that are responsible, but one of Earth's own creatures.

Before the appearance of humanity, there were more species on the planet than at the time of the dinosaurs—a remarkable recovery, whose significance we shall return to shortly. But with the advent of human beings, things began to change. In our early days, we hunted to extinction some of the large animals in North America and in parts of Africa and Asia. Later we eradicated many species simply because they were in our way. And more recently, we have destroyed many more through sheer lack of care.

Current estimates suggest that species are disappearing at the rate of one per hour or perhaps faster! At this rate, more than half the earth's plant and animal species will have been eliminated within the next few hundred years. But, given that our destructive potential accelerates along with our technological "progress," we will probably reach this point much sooner.

On the graph of extinctions, we have already fallen over the precipice. The entire history of humanity occupies less than a thousandth of an inch along the time axis of the graph on page 149. Our own lifetimes correspond to less than a millionth of an inch on this scale. Yet we have already caused a clearly visible drop in the curve.

But the curve need not plummet further. We have not yet entered a full-blown greenhouse effect. The ozone layer has not been destroyed. Not all the forests have disappeared. We need not be, like the dinosaurs, a species that suddenly became extinct—a mere geological relic. There is still hope. We still have the opportunity to redeem ourselves.

Evolutionary Kicks

Even if another mass extinction were to occur, all would not be lost. Evolution would still continue. Indeed, if the past is any indication of what we should expect, it would leap ahead.

Hard-bodied organisms began to flourish only after the mass marine extinction that ended the Pre-Cambrian Era. Amphibians began to colonize the land only after the Devonian extinction, 365 million

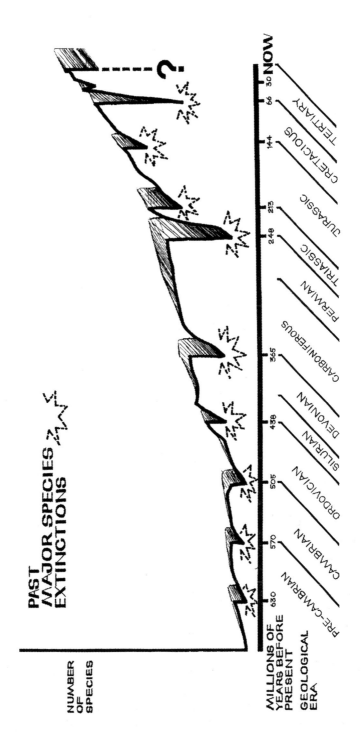

PAST
MAJOR SPECIES
EXTINCTIONS

NUMBER
OF
SPECIES

NOW

TERTIARY

CRETACIOUS

JURASSIC

TRIASSIC

PERMIAN

CARBONIFEROUS

DEVONIAN

SILURIAN

ORDOVICIAN

CAMBRIAN

PRE-CAMBRIAN

MILLIONS OF
YEARS BEFORE
PRESENT

GEOLOGICAL
ERA

30 66 144 213 248 365 438 505 570 630

years ago. And it was the major extinction of 248 million years ago that preceded the appearance of the first dinosaurs.

The catastrophe that ended the dinosaurs' reign led in turn to the evolution of mammals. Small, rodent-like mammals did already exist, but had not evolved very fast. The fact that some of them lived in burrows probably helped them survive whatever environmental catastrophe befell the organisms of those times. Afterward, they evolved very rapidly, diversifying into the wealth of mammal species that we now know—including ourselves.

The reason for this sudden burst of evolutionary activity is easy to understand. Before the catastrophe, the ecological system would have been in a stable state; most species would have had plenty of time to become well adapted to their environment. There would have been little pressure for evolutionary change.

After a mass extinction, things would have been very different. The living matrix of the biosphere would have changed profoundly. Most species that survived would have found themselves in circumstances to which they were not as well suited: sources of food may have disappeared, the climate may have changed, new dangers may have emerged. In this new ecological context, life would have been under renewed pressure to evolve. New adaptations would establish themselves quickly and new species would proliferate.

In short, the curve of evolution would have leapt upward once more.

The Upside of Extinction

Mass extinctions can therefore have a positive side. If the dinosaurs had not disappeared when they did, mammals might have remained rodents and human beings would never have been born. In this respect, we have good reason to be thankful for the disaster of 66 million years ago.

And, should it turn out that humanity's activities do result in another decimation of the planet's species, who is to say what new evolutionary opportunities this might create? The dinosaurs would never have guessed that mammals, human beings, and civilization would follow them. Who knows what phoenix could arise from our ashes?

Whatever form they might take, the species that followed our demise might be very grateful to us for having set the stage and for creating the evolutionary opportunity they needed.

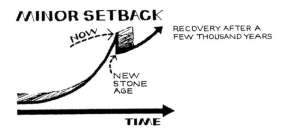

MINOR SETBACK

NOW →

RECOVERY AFTER A FEW THOUSAND YEARS

NEW STONE AGE

TIME

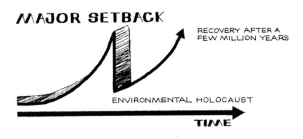

MAJOR SETBACK

RECOVERY AFTER A FEW MILLION YEARS

ENVIRONMENTAL HOLOCAUST

TIME

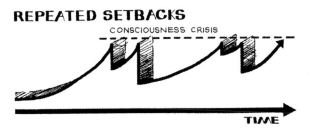

REPEATED SETBACKS

CONSCIOUSNESS CRISIS

TIME

Knocking on Heaven's Door

After such a setback, evolution would resume its steady march toward greater complexity and higher order. It would also resume its steady acceleration, though initially at a much slower pace.

If we were to set ourselves back fifty thousand years to some "New Stone Age," our progress would be slowed considerably. However, as we once again strove to improve our lot, each new advance would serve as a platform for further advances, leading, as before, to an increasing rate of development.

Moreover, although such a calamity might set us back considerably in our material progress, our internal progress would not be so badly affected. It seems probable that we would retain some of the knowledge, understanding, learning, and awareness that we have accumulated, giving us a head start over our Stone Age predecessors. We could then find ourselves entering a new technological age in centuries rather than millennia—though, hopefully, with more wisdom than before.

Even if some environmental holocaust were to wipe us out completely, biological evolution would continue. Inevitably, though slowly, new species would emerge. Novel qualities and abilities would appear, all serving as platforms for further evolutionary advance. Slowly but surely, evolution would continue its inexorable acceleration.

Given the evolutionary trend toward higher orders of information processing, it is very likely that creatures with large and complex nervous systems would again emerge. Eventually, beings with an intelligence similar to or surpassing our own might appear. Such beings might develop symbolic language through which to share their discoveries, and if they had hands, or some other way of manipulating their environment, they could develop technology.

If they remained stuck in a self-centered mode of consciousness, life on Earth would again come under increasing pressure. The planet would be in another crisis of consciousness. And, if this species could not raise its level of awareness, evolution might again be thrown back another fifty thousand, or even fifty million, years.

Then, once more, it would resume its relentless climb toward higher levels of organization and higher rates of change. And once more it would face an inner challenge.

Again and again, life would be confronted by the same challenge, the same intelligence test. Again and again, it would have to answer the same crucial questions. Is this a being that can awaken to its inner world as fully as it has to the physical world? Is this a species that can make the leap into conscious evolution and a higher order of intelligence?

These are the questions facing us today: Are we ready to make that leap? Can we use our gifts of understanding, creativity, and choice in our true self-interest? Can we use our growing freedom from physical constraints to liberate our minds from outdated attitudes and beliefs? Can we develop a new, more enlightened mode of consciousness?

And if we do, what lies ahead? It turns out that it may not be quite what we expect. Indeed, it may be very different from anything we have ever dared imagine.

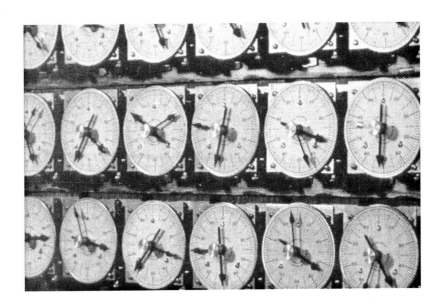

Compression –
The Collapse of Time

"Now! Now!" cried the Queen. "Faster! Faster!"

— Lewis Carroll

Let us suppose, then, that humanity survives these critical times and continues to evolve. What might the future look like then?

One thing is clear: Change will occur faster and faster. Much of this change will occur at the leading edge of our current technologies. Computers will become faster, smaller, and more powerful. Scientists today are talking of optical computers working at the speed of light, quantum computers storing information in individual atoms and millions of times smaller than today's, and "wet" computers using DNA or other biological components that may offer true

153

artificial intelligence. Whatever the technology, the computers of the future will have left current computers far behind.

Since the birth of the microprocessor in 1971, microprocessor performance has increased 25,000 times. If this pattern continues, a personal computer of 2020 will be as powerful as all the computers in Silicon Valley in 1998. Fantastic? Yes, but if someone had told me thirty years ago that I would be carrying the entire computing capacity of Great Britain in a briefcase, I would probably have scoffed.

Such extraordinary increases in computing power and speed will change how we communicate in ways that are impossible to even begin to predict. Remember that in 199, when the World Wide Web was first introduced, no one, not even its originators, had any idea that it would take off as it has.

However, in addition to these and other remarkable technological developments, many of which may build on inventions or discoveries that we cannot possibly foresee today, there is another area of progress that could become even more significant, and could outpace our accelerating technological development. This is the development of the human mind and spirit.

Looking back over human history, we can see how we have progressed from hunting-gathering groups into agricultural communities, followed by the transition to the Industrial Age, and now to the Information Age. There is, however, no reason to suppose that information technology is our final technology; it is just the current focus of our development. I believe the next major transition will be the transition to what we might call the Consciousness Age—a period when the exploration and development of the human mind will become our major focus.

There are two principal reasons for believing this. First, this is the direction in which our current crises are pushing us. As I have already discussed, if we are to survive the critical times we are now passing through, it is essential that we undergo a profound shift in values and awaken to our inner truths and our full spiritual potential. As Buckminster Fuller put it, we are facing our final evolutionary exam. Is the human species fit to survive? Can we develop the consciousness that will allow us to use our prodigious powers with wisdom? If our civilization continues, it will be because we have passed that test, and will have already made the step into the exploration of human consciousness.

Second, inner awakening offers us what we really want. Beneath all our searching, we are looking for an inner well-being—peace of mind, joy, happiness, satisfaction, or however you might identify it. All our material progress is, in one way or another, aimed at fulfilling that inner quest. We may not always see it that way, and may become trapped in the belief that material progress is the goal of life; nevertheless, our ultimate motivation is an inner one. The more we wake up to this fact, the more the focus of our attention will shift from material progress to the means to achieve this inner goal directly. This, as I pointed out earlier, may ultimately be what all our material freedom is for: the freedom to make the transition to this next phase of our evolution.

Inward Acceleration

The Industrial Revolution happened much faster than the Agricultural Revolution, and the Information Revolution faster still. There are several reasons to suppose that if we do make the transition into this new arena of human evolution, progress will take place even more rapidly.

First, inner evolution would represent another step in the direction of ephemeralization, the trend toward doing more with less. Just as it takes less matter and energy to modify a piece of computer software than it does to modify the engine of an automobile, it takes even less to change our thinking.

The obstacles to inner change are not physical but mental. They are our attitudes, our mental habits, our assumptions as to what is possible, and our beliefs as to what we should do. As we learn how to release our minds from these fixations, we could find ourselves changing very rapidly indeed.

Second, as in previous leaps forward, the new arena of progress will make use of previous advances to increase its rate of development. The Information Revolution has stood on the shoulders of the Industrial Revolution, and used the earlier advances of mass production, transportation, distribution, project management, and other skills and technologies to its own advantage. A similar phenomenon is happening with the exploration and development of human consciousness.

Information technology is speeding the evolution of consciousness in a number of ways. Books, one of the oldest information technologies, are having a major impact. Thirty years ago, when I first became interested in spiritual affairs, the bookstores in Cambridge, England—some of the largest and most comprehensive bookstores in the country—had only a shelf or two dedicated to personal development. Today, most cities in the developed nations have specialized bookstores dedicated to consciousness, self-development, and spirituality. The "New Age" market has long been one of the fastest-expanding sectors of publishing; and for the the last decade or more, books that are concerned in one way or another with inner growth top ten on *The New York Times'* bestseller list.

On television, there are an increasing number of programs focusing on health, healing, spiritual wisdom, and the like. Screenwriters now sneak spiritual themes into their scripts: *The Matrix* trilogy, for example, suggests that we live in a radically illusory world, which is in some ways reminiscent of the Vedanta concept of *maya* that points to the unreality of what we take to be the physical world. Popular music lyrics repeatedly challenge the existing materialistic mindset, encouraging people to break free from their cultural conditioning. DVDs and audiotapes mean that anyone can have access to spiritual wisdom from around the world.

The Internet is overflowing with sites dedicated to the transformation of consciousness. There are thousands upon thousands of Web pages offering advice, experience, techniques, and links to other such sites. And the number is growing daily. It may be that, just as the greatest unexpected spinoff from the Apollo 12 mission to the moon was the photographs of the earth that the astronauts brought back, the most unexpected contribution of the Internet to world affairs will turn out to be the facilitation of our inner, spiritual evolution.

The net result of all of this cross-fertilization is that we no longer have to learn the art of self-liberation from scratch, through a somewhat "hit-or-miss" approach. We can learn from each other how best to move toward a more mature mode of being. Once again, positive-feedback loops are at work.

The more we awaken to our inner selves, the more free our minds will become. The more free we become in ourselves, the more creative we can be. And the more creative we become, the better we can apply ourselves to the task of inner awakening.

The more we discover about our own inner liberation, the more we will have to offer others in their awakening. The more they awaken, the more we will benefit. As this positive feedback continues to accelerate, we may find that the maturation and inner growth we now expect in a lifetime could happen in years.

Moreover, we are all standing on the spiritual shoulders of those who have gone before. The more fully adults awaken from their dreams, the less likely they are to infect their children with the erroneous thinking and value system that so troubles our world. Not having so much conditioning to unlearn as their parents did, the next generation could mature that much more quickly.

Already there are signs that this is happening. I know many in their teens and early twenties whose perceptions and values far outshine the liberated thinking of a couple of decades ago. Those of us who lived through the halcyon days of the sixties may have thought our philosophy of life was pretty cool; by the standards of the time, it probably was. But place some of the wiser kids of today back in that world, and they would stand out as beacons of wisdom.

The net result of these feedback loops is that spiritual evolution will wind itself into ever-faster rates of progress as surely as our material evolution has. Moreover, its freedom from material constraints could lead to an acceleration in development that far outstrips our current rates of technological progress.

A Blind Spot on the Future

Because we find it difficult to entertain the idea of an ever-growing pace of life, most of us have developed a blind spot about the future. We can imagine how things will be if they keep on changing as they are now—and even that can make us pretty dizzy—but we find it hard to picture a world in which change keeps coming faster. As a result, we overlook, or ignore, the full consequences of this trend.

Most future scenarios, whether devised by corporate strategists, government think tanks, or science fiction writers, generally assume that the pace of development will be similar to the pace today, or perhaps a little faster. Seldom do forecasters consider the full impact of continued exponential acceleration.

In the early 1950s, for example, eminent scientists were predicting that it would take at least fifty years to put a person on the moon, primarily because it would take that long to make all the necessary technological advances. They underestimated the increased rates of progress that led to the fulfillment of this goal in only fifteen years.

In a similar way, the growth of information technology has been consistently underestimated. The TV series *Star Trek* was conceived as happening two hundred years in the future, by which time computers would no longer use magnetic tape and would synthesize human speech. We may not yet have boldly gone beyond our own solar system, but as far as computers are concerned, reality caught up with fantasy in less than twenty years.

There is no reason to believe that we are not making similar errors today. If we do survive these challenging times and move on in our evolution, it seems more than probable that the pace of change will continue to quicken, and any predictions we may make are likely to materialize far faster than we anticipate.

The implications of such sustained acceleration are quite staggering. The degree of progress that humanity has experienced in the two hundred years since the Industrial Revolution is similar to—possibly greater than—the degree of progress that occurred over the preceding two thousand years. This, in turn, was of a magnitude similar to or greater than the progress of the previous twenty thousand years.

If rates of development continue to speed up, we could see such degrees of progress compressed into a few decades.

And then to mere years.

And after that . . . ?

Who knows—we could experience as many leaps in our own lifetimes as have occurred in the whole of our evolution so far.

Singularities —
The Shape of the Future

Now there is more "now" than there was even a few months ago, and even more "now" is on the way.

—ET 101

As we saw in the first chapter, accelerating change is a pattern that runs throughout the history of evolution. The Big Bang happened twelve billion years ago (give or take a couple of billion years). The evolution of simple life forms began four billion years ago. Multicellular life appeared a billion or so years ago. The evolution of complex nervous systems, made possible by the emergence of vertebrates, began several hundred million years ago. Mammals appeared tens of millions of years ago. The genus *Homo* first stood on the planet a couple of million years ago. *Homo sapiens* appeared several hundred thousand years ago. The shift to *Homo sapiens sapiens* that was triggered by the emergence of language and tool use, and which resulted in the Agricultural Revolution, began tens of thousands of years ago. Civilization—the movement into towns and cities— started several thousand years ago. The Industrial Revolution began a few centuries ago. And the Information Revolution is but a few decades old.

Each new development has occurred in a fraction of the time of the previous one—somewhere between one-quarter and one-tenth the time.

The stages of evolution that I've chosen here are, of course, somewhat arbitrary. One could argue that other events marked equally significant leaps forward, or that some that have been included should be dropped. This would lead to different lengths of time and to different ratios between them. But however one chooses the significant markers, the pattern is generally the same: the intervals get shorter and shorter.

If evolution continues to follow this pattern in the future (and we have seen there are good reasons to suppose it will), then future developments will happen more quickly. The intervals will drop from decades to years to months. We would be heading toward a moment when the intervals decrease to zero, and the rate of change becomes infinite. This is the possible singularity I referred to earlier: a point where the equations break down and cease to have any meaning.

A simple mathematical example is the series $1/2+1/4+1/8+1/16+1/32+1/64+$ . . . (the three dots are a mathematician's way of indicating that the series goes on forever). You might think that if you keep on adding more terms to the series, each one half the size of the preceding term, you could make the final sum as large as you like; but it turns out that however many terms you add, the total sum will get closer and closer to 2, but never actually get there. The series is said to tend toward a limit (in this case the limit is 2). In a similar way, if major developments continue to occur in shorter and shorter times, there will be a corresponding time limit to our evolutionary progress. This does not mean there will be a limit to how much evolution we can experience—the opposite, in fact. We would find ourselves evolving so fast that we experience an unimaginable degree of evolution within a finite time. The time limit would be the date in the future when our rate of development becomes infinitely rapid.

The Singularity

When might this moment occur? People such as Vernor Vinge, who chart the acceleration of technological development, argue for a date somewhere around the year 2035. They believe the trigger for the singularity will be the development of the superintelligent computer. Although current computers are very fast by human standards, they are still not nearly as complex as our own brains. In terms of sheer processing capacity, the human brain, with its tens of billions of neurons, is about a million times more powerful than a computer. That is why you and I can easily pick out a person from a background of trees and buildings, and recognize them as someone we know, all in a fraction of a second, while a robot still has a hard time following the white line down the middle of the road.

However, if computing power keeps doubling every eighteen months, as it has done for the last twenty years, then some time in the 2030s there will be computers that can equal the human brain's abilities. From there, it is only a small step to the computer that can surpass the human brain. There would then be little point in human beings' designing future computers; superintelligent machines would be able to design better ones, and do so faster. Once superintelligent machines, rather than human beings, drove the rate of progress, an exponential runaway effect would be created. Computer power would no longer be doubling once every eighteen months. A simple mathematical analysis shows that superintelligent computers designing even more intelligent machines, which in turn could design yet more intelligent machines, would cause the doubling time to drop from eighteen months to nine months, to four-and-a-half months, to nine weeks, to thirty days, to fifteen days. . . . Another two weeks after that, computing power would have reached infinity. We would have arrived at a singularity—the point at which the mathematical equations break down and the old laws no longer apply.

Such a scenario is based on technological development alone. But, as I argued in the previous chapter, there is good reason to believe that before we arrive at some such technological singularity we will have already moved into the next phase of evolution, the development of human consciousness. Once it takes hold, inner development is likely to progress even more rapidly than technological development. We could arrive at a spiritual singularity—a moment of unimaginably rapid inner awakening—before we reached any technological singularity.

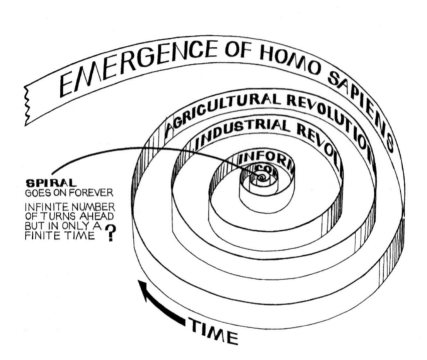

Timewave Zero

Other analyses of historical trends also point to a possible singularity occurring sometime in the next half-century. One approach was that of the deceased American philosopher of science Terence McKenna. He has developed a fractal mathematical function that, he claims, charts the overall rate of ingression of novelty into the world. The curve that results is not a smooth curve, but one that has peaks and troughs corresponding to the peaks and troughs of human history.[2]

---

[2] A good summary of McKenna's ideas can be found in the journal *ReVISION*, vol. 10:1, Summer 1987.

The most significant characteristic of McKenna's timewave is that the shape repeats itself, but over shorter and shorter intervals of time. The curve shows a surge in novelty between 15,000 and 8,000 B.C., corresponding to the approximate dates of the Neolithic Age and the emergence of agriculture. Exactly the same pattern is repeated, although sixty-four times faster, from A.D. 1750 to 1825—the period known as the European Enlightenment and the beginning of the Industrial Era.

Another surge of novelty occurred around 500 B.C. This was the time when Lao-Tzu, Plato, Zoroaster, Buddha, and others, who would have a major influence on the millennia ahead, appeared in the world. It saw the rise of ancient Greece and the beginnings of European culture. This surge continued for several centuries, then slowed down in the fourth century A.D. with the fall of Rome, and finally sputtered to an end with the onset of the Dark Ages. The repeating nature of McKenna's timewave shows the same pattern recurring in the twentieth century, from 1967 through to the early 1990s—again, sixty-four times as fast as before. Later, around 2010, it repeats again, sixty-four times faster still.

This repeating historical pattern corresponds to a series in which each additional term is one-sixty-fourth the length of the previous one. The series has an infinite number of terms, but as with other series of this type its sum is finite. That is to say, it comes to a definite end, a time when the cycles of change are compressed from years to months to weeks to days to . . . McKenna calls this point "Timewave Zero." Its date, according to his calculations, is December 21, 2012.

The year 2012 seems frighteningly close. One's immediate response might be that rates of change could not become that fast in so short a time. Yet we should not forget that when estimating the pace of the future we tend to think in terms of today's pace, and our initial projections nearly always fall short. Many as yet unforeseen advances and revolutions could take the rate of change far beyond what we now imagine possible.

We should also remember that it would not be material progress that would be moving so fast, but our inner spiritual development.

An Evolutionary Asymptote?

Needless to say, McKenna's formula is only one possible model of the curve of human history. My own approach has been to try to fit various mathematical curves to our evolutionary progress and see where the curve is heading. Such attempts inevitably involve a number of assumptions. How, for example, do we measure "progress"? Should we count social and political innovations such as the welfare state along with scientific discoveries and technological breakthroughs? And what values should be assigned to particular advances? Was the invention of photocopying as significant as that of the printing press?

Even having chosen a set of significant steps and plotted them as a graph, it is still not easy to see what type of function describes the curve. There certainly are mathematical techniques for deciding how well an equation fits a curve. But having found a "best fit," the possibility always remains that some untried type of function might fit even better.

Over the years, I have tried many different sets of data and many different functions. The result is a variety of graphs, each approximating the pattern of human evolution, but none exact or definitive. Even so, nearly all of them have one trend in common. Sooner or later they become asymptotic—that is to say, the curve goes vertical, signifying an infinitely fast rate of change. Some have their asymptote in the near future; others have it a century or two ahead.

We are led to a startling and mind-boggling conclusion: If we survive our present challenges and our rate of development keeps on accelerating, we are not going to continue evolving for eons into the future. We could see the whole of our future evolution—as much development as we can conceive of, and more—compressed into a century or less. Within a few generations, perhaps within our own lifetimes, we could reach the end of our evolutionary journey.

Within a finite time we could taste infinity.

Coping with Compression

There are, of course, many reasons why we may not reach the final stages of compression. First we have to steer our way through our current set of crises. And even if we do survive these challenges, we may well discover further testing points ahead. If we fail to respond to them appropriately, we might find ourselves set back to some earlier, and slower, phase of evolution.

There is also the question of whether our minds could tolerate ever-increasing change. We might, for example, be able to cope with a pace double that of today, and possibly a pace ten times as fast. But what about a hundred times, or a thousand times? Is there an ultimate limit to how fast the human mind and body can adapt?

From our current mode of consciousness, it may be very hard to imagine ourselves coping with such astronomical rates of change. But who knows what might be possible once our minds are liberated from their attachment to material things? We may relate to change in a very different way, and our minds may then operate at a very different pace.

An example of this sometimes occurs at the point of death. Relieved of its ties to the senses, the mind seems to function at an altogether different speed. People who have had a brush with death often report seeing their entire lives flash before their eyes. In clock time, the review may last only a second or so, but in that moment they can relive years of experience.

Finally, we should recall that our future evolutionary progress is likely to be less material in nature. If we do come through these troubled times and continue with our development, it will be our perceptions, our attitudes, our thinking, and our awareness that will be changing faster and faster, not necessarily the world around us. We will be experiencing an ever-accelerating inner awakening. This may turn out to be far easier to handle than ever-accelerating material change. Indeed, we would probably welcome it.

Omega –
A White Hole in Time

The day will come when, after harnessing the winds, the tides and gravitation, we shall harness for God the energies of Love. And on that day, for the second time in the history of the world, man will have discovered fire.

—Teilhard de Chardin

The acceleration of evolution toward a time of infinitely rapid change is not so exceptional as one might at first suppose. The evolution of matter in a star follows a similar pattern.

For 99.99 percent of its existence, a star burns hydrogen, fusing the atoms into helium and radiating the released energy as light. Eventually the hydrogen runs out. For a star the size of our sun, this

167

happens after about 10 billion years; it is currently about halfway through its life. Larger stars burn up more quickly; smaller ones can last as long as 100 billion years.

When all the hydrogen has been consumed, a star can, if it is sufficiently massive, switch to burning the helium it has created, transforming it into carbon. This keeps the star going for another million years or so. When the helium is used up, the star can survive for another thousand years by fusing the carbon into neon. And when the carbon runs out, the star burns the neon to form silicon. But the neon is exhausted within a year. Then, in a process that lasts only a few days, the silicon fuses into iron.

That is as far as a star can go along this particular path. Fusing iron does not release energy; it requires additional energy. The star's fire begins to die, and with it the energy that until now has supported the weight of its outer layers. Very quickly, it begins to collapse.

As its matter becomes increasingly compressed, its gravitational field increases. Within minutes it becomes so intense that even atoms cannot withstand the pressure. Electrons are stripped away and atomic nuclei pack in on each other, reaching densities of more than a million tons per cubic inch. This disintegration releases enormous amounts of energy, blowing off the star's outer layers in what is known as a supernova. This is one of the Universe's more spectacular shows, more energy being released during these few seconds than over the rest of the star's entire life.

Left behind is a neutron star: a solid mass of neutrons a mere fifteen or so miles across. For a sufficiently massive star (one about three times the mass of the sun), the gravitational field has now become so strong that matter itself breaks down. The star is said to have reached a singularity: a point at which the laws of physics no longer work. Mathematical equations become filled with zeros and infinities and cease to make any sense. There is a hole in space.

So intense is the gravitational field that nothing can escape it. Even light is pulled back down. If no light can escape, then nothing can be seen of the star. It becomes a *black hole*.

The Gravity of Love

The parallels between the evolution of a star and the pattern we have traced in the evolution of humanity are intriguing. Not only do both show an accelerating pattern of development; the factors behind this acceleration are analogous.

Whereas a star's matter is pulled together by the force of gravity, a species such as ourselves is pulled forward by our search for a more satisfying inner state. Our minds gravitate toward inner peace. We may not at first see this to be our goal. Caught up in our material desires, we may believe it is comfort, security, or some other worldly satisfaction that we want. But the closer we draw to our own center, the clearer it becomes that, beneath everything, we are seeking inner peace and love. And the more we recognize our true goal, the faster we are able to move toward it.

In this regard, gravity and love are not that different. Gravity is the attraction of mass for itself. It is a force that pulls the physical Universe back toward its original unity. Similarly, love can be considered as the attraction of life for itself—the desire for conscious union with another. Its ultimate expression is reunion with our own source, with the essence of our consciousness. It is this that is pulling us faster and faster along our evolutionary curve toward a singularity in time. Buckminster Fuller summed it up poetically in his revised Lord's Prayer: "Love," he wrote, "is metaphysical gravity."

The Time Horizon

Another similarity between stellar evolution and our own conscious evolution concerns the *event horizon* that surrounds a black hole. The event horizon is the boundary around the star within which the gravitational force is so strong that not even light can escape. Since nothing can travel faster than light, there is no way any information can get out across this boundary. The result is that you can see nothing of events taking place on the other side of the event horizon.

A parallel horizon could well exist for humanity, except that this time it would be a horizon in time rather than one in space. A thousand years ago, change was much slower and the future a hundred years on would not have been markedly different. By the time of the Industrial Revolution, the pace of life had increased dramatically, making it much more difficult to foretell the future a hundred years ahead. But it would still have been possible to look a decade or two into the future with reasonable certainty.

Today it is not possible to see even that far ahead. Unforeseen developments mean that we can no longer predict the future of the world more than a few years ahead. So closely are our affairs now interwoven that unexpected events in one person's mind can have reverberations around the world, changing the future for all concerned. And when economies crash without warning, the best-laid plans of machines and men can vanish overnight.

There is, in effect, an information horizon ahead of us, albeit a somewhat fuzzy one. Beyond this horizon, the future will probably be unlike anything we can anticipate. And the faster change occurs, the closer we come to this horizon.

As the predictable future shrinks from decades to years to months and less, there may well come a time when it is difficult to make any forecasts at all. History will have become chaotic—not chaotic in the sense of disorganized, but in the mathematical sense of unpredictable. However much progress we may have made in our inner evolution, it will be impossible for us to be sure what is coming next. Completely unexpected developments could always be just around the corner.

Facing Uncertainty

Having to face increasing uncertainty could play an important role in our inner liberation. As long as we are looking to the future for our fulfillment, uncertainty spells insecurity—and insecurity is something most of us find hard to manage. If we insist on holding on to our fixed views, the changes we encounter will probably drive us crazy. They will incline us more toward setback than breakthrough.

Only through letting go of our need for certainty, and with it our concern for how things might or might not be, will we find the inner stability to see us through such change-filled times. In this regard, ever-accelerating change may be just the trigger we need to shake us to our senses.

Again, one might draw a parallel with the later stages of stellar evolution. In a collapsing star, the ultra-intense gravitational field breaks down the very structure of matter, returning it to its fundamental constituents. With our own inner evolution it may take ultra-intense rates of change to bring about the breakdown of our materialist mindsets and our attachment to the physical world. Increasing time compression could be another factor forcing us to return to the present moment.

The End of Evolution

So where might evolution take us as we head toward this singularity in time?

The great mystic traditions are unanimous in maintaining that liberation of the mind from its attachments, enlightening as it may be, is only the first of many steps of inner awakening. Beyond it are more universal experiences of mind, deeper understandings and richer perspectives of reality leading on to higher states of consciousness.

Is there a highest state of consciousness? Mahayana Buddhism talks of *sahaj samadhi*, the recognition that *all* phenomena are merely consciousness in its various manifestations. Zen Buddhists speak of total nonduality. Hindu texts refer to the highest state of consciousness as unity with Brahman, a state in which one knows the source of all creation and all its levels of manifestation. And Christian mystics talk of oneness with God.

Whether or not these descriptions are referring to exactly the same state of consciousness is a question I will leave to those more qualified than I. Nevertheless, they would all seem to be pointing in the same direction: toward a personal evolutionary zenith.

What would happen if this were to become a collective experience rather than a blessing bestowed on one in a hundred million? Would our collective evolution then come to an end? Could it be that, in much the same way as the destiny of matter in a sufficiently massive star is to become a black hole in space, the destiny of a self-conscious species (should it be sufficiently intelligent) is a "spiritual supernova"? Is this the end toward which we are accelerating? A moment when the light of inner awakening radiates throughout the world? A white hole in time?

Omega Point

One person who believed this was indeed our destiny was the French priest and paleontologist Pierre Teilhard de Chardin. Exploring the evolutionary trends toward greater complexity, connectivity, and consciousness, he argued that humanity was moving toward an "Omega Point"—the full descent of spirit into matter, the fulfillment of our evolution. In the concluding words of his essay *My Universe* he writes:

> Like a vast tide, Being will have engulfed the shifting sands of being. Within a now tranquil ocean, each drop of which, nevertheless, will be conscious of remaining itself, the astonishing adventure of the world will have ended. The dream of every mystic, the eternal pantheist ideal, will have found its full and legitimate satisfaction.

He described the Omega Point as a time when light would blaze across the planet—not physical light, but the light of consciousness.

The difference between Teilhard de Chardin's picture and that presented here lies in the timescales involved. He saw this peak of human evolution as being a long way off: millions of years in the future. But, like many others before and after, he did not fully take the implications of an ever-accelerating pace of development into account. However, shortly before he died, he commented on the impact that radio and television were having on the integration of humanity. Technologies like these, he said, were bringing the Omega Point much closer. Had he lived to see the impact of computers and the Internet, he would probably have seen the Omega Point coming even sooner.

The End of Time

At the Omega Point, our evolution's ever-accelerating trend would at last come to an end. But this would not, it must be emphasized, signify an end to the world, at least not in the sense in which we normally mean it. It would certainly mean an end to our attachment to the world; an end to our dysfunctional attitudes and behavior; an end to the world as we know it now.

Time itself would not end. Our bodies would live on. So would our species. We would be free, at last, to truly enjoy our world. And we might continue that way for a very long while.

Or, who knows, we might find ourselves in a totally different reality. We might, for example, find ourselves stepping beyond the realm of space and time. Many mystics have reported an experience in which consciousness itself is not bound by space and time. Modern physics, too, has shown that time and space are not as absolute as everyday experience leads us to us believe. One of the conclusions of Einstein's Special Theory of Relativity is that light is in some ways more fundamental than either space or time. Could it be that when the light of pure consciousness radiates through humanity, these deeper truths will be manifested in some way? Such a radically different mode of consciousness may be totally beyond our everyday experience, and may seem pure science fiction, but that does not make it impossible.

Whatever may happen, there is another sense in which this full awakening might be an end—an end in the sense of a purpose or goal. Could there be an evolutionary summit toward which evolution has been building since time began? Could there be a hidden purpose to Creation?

Surprisingly—or perhaps not—this is a question that physics has now begun to ponder.

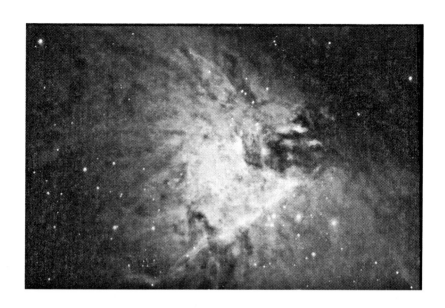

Purpose –
A Design to Creation?

"Any coincidence," said Miss Marple to herself, "is always worth noting. You can throw it away later if it *is* only a coincidence."

—Agatha Christie

P urpose is not something physics usually concerns itself with. It sees the Universe unfolding according to a preordained set of laws. We may not understand all the laws, and even when we do, we may not be able to predict exactly how things will behave, as quantum physics and chaos theory have both made clear. Nonetheless, being physical laws, they leave no room for purpose. At least, not in the sense of striving toward a goal.

However, this is not the only sense in which things can have a purpose. There can also be purpose in design. A clock runs according to well-defined physical laws, but this does not mean it has no purpose. It was constructed and set running in such a way that its movements would have meaning. The question that some scientists are now beginning to ask is: Could the same be true of the Universe? Could it run according to the laws of physics, yet be set up to run in a particular direction, toward a particular end?

A Coincidental Universe?

The way the Universe operates is determined by various fundamental constants such as the masses of the atomic particles, the charge of an electron, and the strength of the gravitational force. Scientists used to think that if one of these constants were to be slightly different, it might make a difference in the way the Universe behaved, but the Universe itself would still exist. They are now realizing that this may not be so. It appears that if the conditions of the original creation had not been exactly as they were, the Universe would not have existed for very long, and life would never have had the chance to evolve.

Physicists believe that at the time of the Big Bang, the number of particles created was very slightly greater than the number of antiparticles: about one part in a billion more. Whenever particles and antiparticles meet, they annihilate each other. Within a short time after the Big Bang, all the antiparticles had met their match and disappeared, along with a corresponding number of particles. But because of the initial inequality, some matter remained. This matter became the Universe we know. Had it not been for this initial imbalance, there would have been no galaxies, no stars, no planets, nor even the simplest of chemical elements.

Moreover, the total number of matter particles left over—about 10^{80} (1 followed by 80 zeros)—was also critical. If the number had been slightly greater, the gravitational forces would have been stronger than the energy of expansion. The young Universe would have rapidly collapsed in on itself to form one huge black hole.

Conversely, if the number had been slightly smaller, gravitational forces would have been weaker, and the Universe would have expanded so rapidly that galaxies would never have had time to form. Again, the Universe as we know it would not have existed.

Another factor crucial for the existence of matter was the mass of the neutron, the particle that together with the proton forms atomic nuclei. If this mass were only 0.2 percent less than its actual value, protons would have rapidly decayed into neutrons and no atoms would ever have been formed.

The atoms that initially formed were hydrogen atoms. However, before these could evolve into the second element, helium, there had to be some other "lucky" coincidences. If the nuclear force, which holds atomic nuclei together against their electromagnetic repulsion, were a few percent weaker, deuterium—a stage that hydrogen passes through as it combines to form helium—would have been very unstable. The Universe would have remained almost pure hydrogen.

If, on the other hand, the nuclear forces had been a few percent stronger, all the hydrogen in the Universe would have burnt to helium in a matter of seconds. And with all the hydrogen gone, there would have been no fuel for stars.

Before helium could evolve into other elements, such as carbon, oxygen, and nitrogen, another coincidence was necessary. The charge on the proton had to be just right. If it had been slightly greater, the nuclei of these heavier atoms would not have been stable. They would have decayed rapidly, leaving a Universe of only hydrogen and helium.

The further evolution of matter into elements heavier than iron had to wait for the first stars to complete their life cycle and turn into supernovae, which released the additional energy that was needed for the synthesis of these larger atoms. But the fact that stars can reach this stage at all depends upon some other fine tunings. If the force of gravity were very slightly stronger, the electromagnetic force very slightly weaker, or the electron slightly less heavy, the convective processes within stars would have been very different. Most stars would have been unable to evolve beyond the stage of burning helium. They would never have reached the supernova stage. And without supernovae, there would have been no heavy elements and thus no possibility of life.

The Coincidence of Life

However, before life could begin, some other very fine tunings were necessary. Life as we know it is based on carbon. All the proteins, amino acids, vitamins, fats, and carbohydrates that make up your body are molecules built on a skeleton of carbon. It was once thought that life based on silicon, or even some other element, might also be possible; but it is now generally believed that only carbon offers the variety and complexity of bonds that living systems depend upon. Yet the very existence of carbon rests on a most precise and unusual coincidence involving a phenomenon known as nuclear resonance. I will not go into the details of this phenomenon, since they involve some more complex physics; put very simply, it determines the probability that a nucleus will capture and combine with the nucleus of another atom. It turns out that if the nuclear resonance level for carbon were not exactly at the value it is, virtually no carbon would ever have formed inside stars and the possibility of life would never have existed.

But this is only half the story. Once a carbon atom does form, there is the possibility of its combining with a helium nucleus to form oxygen. Luckily, however, the nuclear resonance for oxygen lies just below the critical value; otherwise, any carbon that did form would have rapidly disappeared—again making life impossible.

Not only are these two resonances a most remarkable pair of coincidences; they are themselves the result of some very fine tuning between the strengths of nuclear and electromagnetic interactions, along with the relative masses of electrons and protons.

And the list goes on.

The deeper one looks, the more it appears that the initial conditions of the cosmos, the strength of the "bang," and the values of nature's fundamental constants were precisely those required to produce a physical Universe that was stable, that would evolve into a diversity of chemical elements, and that would eventually be able to sustain life.

The Anthropic Principle

How does one make sense of this remarkable collection of coincidences? Has some superintelligence been at work adjusting the laws of physics in order to create the Universe the way it is? Or are they all just coincidences, however remarkable?

Scientists' attempts to answer such questions have given rise to what is known as the Anthropic Principle. In its most general form, this states that the only Universe that can contain human beings (*anthropos* in Greek)—and hence the only Universe that we can observe—is one in which these coincidences are exactly as they are. If they were not, we would not be here to notice the fact.

It may sound simple, but the principle is open to some radically differing interpretations. What is known as the Weak Anthropic Principle falls very much into line with the conventional scientific paradigm, which excludes any notion of a "grand design"—let alone any "Grand Old Designer." It proposes that our very existence as human beings determines the type of Universe we can observe. It is not so much an accident that all the parameters are exactly as they are; it is an inevitability. We cannot possibly know of any other types of Universe, because we would not be around to observe them.

Some proponents of this view hold that there may in fact be numerous other Universes existing in parallel with our own. Others suggest there have been numerous Universes preceding ours and that numerous others have yet to follow. In each of these other Universes, the fundamental constants might well be different. Only in a minute fraction of them, probably less than one in a billion, would the conditions be right for life to evolve. All others would be devoid of life, devoid of intelligent observers, and thus forever unknowable.

This, however, raises the question of whether or not an unknowable Universe can be said to exist. In an attempt to deal with this philosophical problem, and also to handle some of the stranger coincidences that are harder to explain by the Weak Anthropic Principle, cosmologists such as Fred Hoyle in England and John Wheeler in the U.S. have developed an alternative Strong Anthropic Principle. They argue that there can be no matter without an observer, for only when you make an observation do you convert the probability functions of quantum mechanics into actualities. Thus the only Universes that can exist are those that can be observed.

This implies that the initial conditions of any Universe *must be* such that

1. The Universe can continue in a stable form.

2. It continues long enough, and with the right conditions, for life to emerge.

3. Life is able to evolve intelligent beings capable of observing the Universe.

In other words, the Universe exists so that it can be known.

Knowing –
A Conscious Universe

From joy all beings are born,
By joy they are all sustained,
And into joy they again return.

—Taittiriya Upanishad

In the first part of this book, we saw that the gathering and process-ing of information has been one of the principal threads of evolution. The first breakthrough was DNA, which gave matter the ability to store and reproduce information, and became the molecular data bank of life. Later, sexual reproduction allowed two organisms to share their genetic material, speeding up a thousandfold the rate at which Life's growing body of data could be processed and built upon.

181

As living systems evolved, they learned to detect changes in their environment. Nervous systems emerged, processing this sensory data and integrating it into a coherent model of the world. The nervous systems of some creatures became so large that they were able to perform the very complex information processing necessary for symbolic language. Such creatures could share their learnings with each other, and think about the world they saw. They began to form concepts, establish general principles, and thus construct a picture of the world in which they found themselves. Nature had begun to know itself.

Thus began our quest for meaning. We became hungry for knowledge, asking no end of questions in our search for understanding. We even thought about the very process of knowing, and to ensure that our knowledge was reliable, we organized our quest into the disciplines of science.

Our ability to mold the world into new forms led to tools and technologies that added to our powers of knowing. No longer did we have to rely only on our own senses. We created electron microscopes, radio telescopes, X-ray cameras, mass spectrometers, and bubble chambers. We peered into the depths of matter and out into the further reaches of space. How did the Universe come to be? How does it function? Where is it going?

Now, after millennia of seeking, we seem to be closing in on some of the answers. We can look out to the edges of the Universe, back to times when the first galaxies were forming; we can begin to understand how it all started and how it has developed. We have looked back over the history of life on Earth and put together a picture of the way we came to be. We have discovered the molecular code in the genes and are piecing together the hundred million instructions of our own biological program. We have realized that space and time are manifestations of a deeper underlying continuum, and that matter and energy are similarly related. And we seem, at last, to be approaching a unified field theory: an integrated understanding of all the fundamental forces of nature in a single set of mathematical equations.

Needless to say, there is still much that we do not know. And much of what we think we know may later prove only an approximation of the truth. But given the amount of knowledge we have gathered in just a few centuries, particularly in the last few decades, it seems unlikely that another million years will have to pass before our knowing is complete. Cross-fertilization and positive feedback will ensure that our rate of progress in this direction continues to accelerate. We could learn as much in the next twenty years as in the last two thousand.

Inner Knowing

The Strong Anthropic Principle suggests that the Universe has to be one that can come to know itself. If so, it is unlikely that this knowing would be restricted to its physical manifestations. The equally real—in some respects more real—realm of the mind is also waiting to be known.

As self-conscious entities, we can take that inner step. We are aware of our thoughts and feelings. We are conscious of our knowledge, and conscious to some extent of the Self that knows. However, compared to our understanding of the world around us, our knowledge of this inner realm is at present much more thinly spread.

We do know that more is possible. Sprinkled through history, there have been those who have awakened to this inner realm in all its glory. They have come to know the essence of consciousness, and in doing so have realized that this inner essence is the essence of all creation. In the language of Indian philosophy, they have come to know that *Atman*, the consciousness that manifests within us all, is *Brahman*, the source and essence of all Creation.

The vast majority of us may still be far from such realization. But it is the direction we are headed in, both as individuals and as a species. And, as we have seen, there are good reasons to believe that our inner awakening need not take a lot of time. We could, if we put our minds to it, find ourselves fulfilling this inner quest within a century or so—or even less.

Then Brahman would know Itself in all Its dimensions. Through our perception and understanding, It would have come to know Its physical manifestations in all their depth and beauty. And through our own inner explorations, It would have come to know the many manifestations of mind, including the Self, the pure consciousness that underlies all knowing. Life's long journey of data gathering, information processing, knowing, and understanding would be complete. Through us, the Universe would have fulfilled the purpose of its design.

A Universe of Knowing

This is not to imply that the fulfillment of this function rests with human beings alone. As far as we know, there is nothing unique about planet Earth. If the conditions here are right for life, they are almost certainly right on many other planets.

There are over ten billion stars in our galaxy, and if only one-tenth of one per cent of those have planets with the right conditions for life, there are still ten million suitable planets in our galaxy alone. And there are, according to current estimates, a billion other galaxies out there. That means there could be ten million billion planets capable of supporting life!

How many of these planets actually have life on them? Possibly the majority of them. The fact that life on Earth got started soon after the conditions here were right suggests that life probably takes hold wherever it can. If so, the Universe must be teeming with life.

Moreover, the Strong Anthropic Principle postulates that the Universe is set up not only so that life can emerge, but also so that the conscious observers may evolve. If so, the Universe may be teeming with intelligence as well. There may be billions of other self-conscious species out there, all in their own ways discovering both the fullness and the essence of Creation, each and every one of them an opportunity for cosmic self-discovery.

They may not all be at the same stage as we are. Life on many planets may still be at the equivalent of bacteria or simple sponges. On others, it may have passed our phase long ago. And on some, evolution may have reached a similar stage to that on Earth.

From this perspective, we are not, after all, that significant. No more than a single bud in a rose garden.

From the perspective of planet Earth, however, we are most significant. After billions of years, a creature has arisen that has transcended biological evolution. It is our minds, not our bodies, that are evolving. We are a species that can explore and study its world; a species that looks for meaning. We are a species with self-consciousness; a species that knows that it knows.

We are the most creative, most intelligent, and most thoughtful creature the Earth has ever seen. And we have the potential to be much, much more.

Could we be the moment Earth has been waiting for?

The End –
Or the Beginning?

May you live in interesting times.

—Old Chinese Curse

Whether or not this particular species on planet Earth will be able to blossom into full knowing is still an open question. We are an evolutionary seed, cast into the winds of space and time. Whether or not we become all that we may be is up to us. We have been given every opportunity and facility. But we have also been given the reins of our own destiny.

We are, in effect, facing an evolutionary exam, a cosmic intelligence test. We have prodigious powers at our disposal—enough to harm a planet—and before we can continue our evolutionary journey we must prove that we have the wisdom to use these powers for the benefit of all.

This trial may not be unique to humankind on planet Earth. Any intelligent, tool-using life form will probably meet a similar test. A species that can modify its environment will almost certainly want to use its creativity to improve its chances of survival. Doubtless it would be delighted with a longer life expectancy, and might not, at first, see any need to curb its biological productivity. Slowly, imperceptibly at first, its population would begin to grow.

So also would its technological abilities. As with any other evolutionary process, each new advance would facilitate further advances. Its rate of development would accelerate, and if it were not careful it could find itself changing its world faster than its planetary biosystem could adjust.

Whether such a species would fall into the trap of self-centeredness is an open question. If it did not, it might develop the wisdom and the will to manage its growing powers and thus avoid catastrophe. But a technological species whose psychological development followed a course similar to ours would probably find itself facing a parallel crisis of consciousness. If it were to survive, then it too would need to transcend its self-centeredness.

Any intelligent tool-using species enters what is, in effect, a window in time. The window opens with the emergence of self-consciousness. The species then embarks on a dash through history. Can its inner evolution keep pace with its material development? Can it make it through to a full awakening of consciousness before the side effects of misguided creativity force the window closed?

The window in time that opened when life on Earth took the leap into *Homo sapiens sapiens* is at the point of closing. We are in the last moments of our 50,000-year dash: a dash from emerging consciousness to full enlightenment. In the words of the verses with which this book opened, we are W. B. Yeats' rough beast, our hour come round at last, racing against time itself to be born.

Mount Washington summit,
Full Moon at its north node and closest approach to Earth,
the largest and most brilliant of Moons,
Mars alongside, also at its brightest,
a trail of flight cleaving the two,
Capricorn guarding, lives changing,
governments talking of war,
business talking of new paradigms,
old enemies connecting, shaking hands beneath the sea,
temporally synchronistic sandwiches playing through our lives,
the end of a journey,
the end of the workbook,
thankful for many blessings,
at peace for a while,
wondering whether we can all be friends,
remembering the real work
and the choice we each must make
— remembering not to worry.

188

Index

Bernard, Claude, 31
Bhagavad Gita, 92
Bible, the, 26, 90
Big Bang, 5, 159, 176
Black hole, 168, 169, 171, 176
Blake, William, 90
Blind spot on future, 157–158
Blood, warm, 126–127
Brahman, 171, 183
Brain. *See also* Consciousness;
    Mind
    capacities of, 135–136
    and capacity for language, 18
    vs. computer, 161
    evolution of, 14–15
Brazil, 43
Breeding, selective, 22
A Brief History of Time (Hawking),
    ix
Buddha, the, 89, 96–97, 110
Buddhism, 96–97, 141, 171

Campbell, Joseph, 139
Cancers, 47, 55–57
Carbon, 168, 177, 178
Carbon dioxide, 126
    overproduction of, 44, 45, 146
Caritas, 111
Carroll, Lewis, 35, 153
CFCs, 47–48, 49
Change
    acceleration of, ix, x, 3–5, 9–10,
        12, 24, 28–29, 35–36, 76,
        79–80, 81, 153–154,
        157–158, 169–170
    coping with, 49, 76, 79–80, 81,
        164–165, 170–171
    creation of stress by, 79–80
    fear of, 71, 75–76
    and feedback, 12, 23, 26, 35–36
    resistance to, 75–76
    and satisfaction of inner needs,
        60–61
    in technology, 3, 4, 7, 10,
        23–24, 26, 153–154
    unexpected, 49, 170

Channeling, 86
Children, innocence of, 121
Chimpanzees, 17, 18, 21
Chlorofluorocarbon (CFC) gases,
    47–48, 49
Christianity
    and enlightenment, 97, 171
    prophecy in, 141–144
Christie, Agatha, 175
Clark, Kenneth, 90
Climate, 44–46, 49, 147
Coincidence
    life as, 176, 178, 179
    universe as, 176–177, 178–179
Cold-blooded animals, 127
Coleridge, Samuel Taylor, 40
Communications
    development of, 25–26
    ephemeralization of, 27
    and global integration, 28–29,
        172
Competition, satisfaction of needs
    through, 69, 122
Compound interest, 12
Computers
    capacity of, 26, 27, 36, 37,
        153–154, 158, 161
    impact of, 37, 172
    production of, 27–28
Conditioning, cultural
    freedom from, 86–87, 88, 115,
        116, 130, 144, 156, 157
    as hypnotic state, 87–88
    into materialism, 68, 85, 143
    obscuring of inner needs by, xii,
        65, 68–69
    obstruction of inner peace by,
        85–86, 87, 96
    as prison, 91
Consciousness
    acceleration of, 155–157, 163
    attachments of, 91, 92, 116,
        136
    detachment of, 91–92, 170–171
    development of, 120–121
    essence of, 183

Ego-mind, *continued*
  and fear, 72–73
  and mistaken behavior, 107
Einstein, Albert, 51, 173
Electricity, 23
El Niño, 43
Emerson, Ralph Waldo, 21, 67
Employment, 128, 129
End of the world, 140, 172
Energy
  capturing of, 33
  harnessing of, 22–24
  levels of consumption of, 42,
    43, 52, 53
  renewable, 52
  sources of, 22–23, 43, 125–127
Enlightenment
  acceleration of, 155–157, 163,
    164–165
  definitions of, 95–96
  in determining the future, 141
  feedback in, 156–157
  levels of, 171
  and maturity, 123
  in meditation, 115, 116–117
  as perceptual shift, 96–98
Environment
  consequences of human error
    for, 79, 145–146
  destruction of, 43–48, 56,
    62, 135, 136, 140, 144,
    145–146
  impact of consumption on,
    42–43
  resistance to behavioral change
    and, 75
  restoration of, 52–53, 130, 148
  stress on, 4, 10, 37
  unexpected changes in, 49
Ephemeralization, 26–28, 155
Epictetus, 77, 97
Eros, 111
Error(s)
  amplification of, 62
  programming, 56–57
ET 101, 159

Event horizon, 169
Evolution
  acceleration of, ix, x, xi, xii, 6,
    7, 8, 10, 11–12, 13, 14, 15,
    22, 23, 24, 159–165, 186
  crisis in, 137–138
  effect of extinctions on,
    150–152
  end of, 164, 171
  toward freedom, 125–129
  and human creativity, 31–34
  individual development as mir-
    ror of, 119–121, 122, 123
  of life forms, 5, 6, 7, 8, 12–15,
    32, 181–182
  of matter, 5, 12–13, 32,
    167–169, 171, 176–177
  purpose of, xiii, 173
  spiritual, 10, 38, 152, 154,
    155–157, 163, 164–165,
    170–171, 186
  technology as instrument of,
    31–33, 186
Evolutionary exam, 154, 185–186
Exploitation, 69–70, 122
Extinctions, 44, 146–152

Failure, fear of, 71, 78
Family, conditioning by, 87, 88
Famines, 142
Fear
  of change, 71, 75–76
  creation of stress by, 78–79
  and ego, 72–73
  expression of, in relationships,
    110
  freedom from, 82, 91, 130
  imprisonment by, 91
  judgment as projection of, 102
  vs. love, 144
  as motive for saving time, 73
  obstruction of inner peace by,
    71–72, 72–73, 78
  of others, 74–75, 101
  physical effects of, 77–78
  voice of, *see* Self-talk

Huxley, Julian, 17
Hydrogen, 5, 167–168, 177
Hypnosis. *See also* Conditioning,
    cultural; Dehypnosis
    clinical vs. cultural, 87–88, 143
    hidden observer in, 86–87

I, 114. *See also* Ego; Ego-mind;
    Self and "Self-" compounds
Ice ages, 45–46
Ideas
    dissemination of, 26, 28
    as evolutionary force, 32
    in individual development, 120
    recording of, 25–26
Identity, 61–62, 113–114
Illumination, 89–91, 95–96. *See also*
    Enlightenment; Light of con-
    sciousness; Spiritual evolution
Indigenous cultures, innocence of,
    121
Industrial Age, 154, 162
Industrial Revolution, 23, 24, 42,
    127–128
Information, processing of, by or-
    ganisms, 14, 18, 181–182
Information Age, 154, 155
Information horizon, 170
Information technology, 10
    development of, 25–26, 158
    ephemeralization of, 27–28
    as evolutionary stage, 154, 155
    and evolution of consciousness,
      155–156
    and freedom, 128
    and global integration, 28–29,
      172
    growth of, 25
Inner knowledge, *see* Knowledge,
    inner
Inner needs, *see* Needs, inner
Inner peace, *see* Peace, inner
Inner space, 38
Innocence, 121
Intelligence

higher, 152
    vs. malignant behavior, 55–56
    as source of crisis, 135–136
International Business Machines
    (IBM), 27
International relations, fear in, 75
Internet, 28–29, 156, 172
Iron, 5, 168
Isherwood, Margaret, 90

Jeanrenaud, Jean-Paul, 44
Jefferies, Richard, 93
Jesus Christ, 142, 143
Joachim of Fiore, 140
John, St., 142–144
Judeo-Christian prophecy, 141–142
Judgment(s)
    distortion of relationships by,
      101–102
    evaluative, 102
    and love, 104, 106
    as prison, 143
    seeing without, 96, 103–104,
      107, 109, 112, 144

Knowledge
    collective, 18–19
    of Creation, 171, 179–180,
      182–183, 184
    growth of, 18–19
    of self, 38, 114, 115
    thirst for, 19, 182–183
Knowledge, inner
    battle of ego against, 143–144
    discovery of, 86, 183
    obstruction by conditioning, 86,
      87

Labor, *see* Work
Labor-saving devices, 128
Language
    human capacity for, 18
    in individual development, 120
    and learning, 18, 19, 127, 182
Larynx, 18

Molecules, 12–13, 126
Moore's Law, 27
Multicellular organisms, 6, 7, 13–14, 137, 159
My Universe (Teilhard de Chardin), 172

Nasrudhin (Sufi "wise fool"), 68
National Airport (Washington, D.C.), 48
Nature
  evolving human relationship with, 120–121
  exploitation of, 69, 122
  vs. human creativity, 32–33
  innocence toward, 121
Neanderthals, 7
Needs, inner
  amplification of, 62
  confusion of outer well-being with, 68–69, 85, 86, 97, 104, 106, 136
  and detachment, 91, 92
  exploitation as response to, 69–70, 122
  fulfillment of, 60–61, 67–68
  relationships as fulfillment of, 100–102
Nervous system, evolution of, 14–15, 159, 182
Neutron star, 168
New Age publishing, 156
Nichol, Maurice, 97
Noble silence, 110
Novelty
  acceleration of, 12, 13, 22, 162
  and human creativity, 31–32
Nuclear resonance, 178
Nuclear war/weapons, 141

Old Testament prophets, 141–142
Omega Point, 171–172
Ontogeny, and phylogeny, 119–120, 123
Opportunity, crisis as, 137, 138
Ordovician Era, 148

Oxygen, 177, 178
  overproduction of, 126, 137
Ozone layer, 148
  destruction of, 47, 53, 62, 146
  holes in, 4, 10, 49

Pain
  avoidance of, 63–64, 69, 129
  effects of hypnosis on, 86
  pleasure in, 65
  transcendence of, 92, 96–97
Past
  preoccupation with, 93, 130
  projection of, onto others, 103
Peace, inner, 63, 64, 65, 104
  changing of perceptions and, 96, 97–98
  and conquest of materialism, 143–144
  direct achievement of, 155
  and experience of the present, 93–94
  and forgiveness, 108
  gravitation toward, 169
  intrinsic quality of, 91
  through love, 106–107, 110, 111
  maintenance of, in adversity, 68–69
  of maturity, 123
  in meditation, 115, 116
  obstruction by cultural conditioning, 85–86, 87, 96
  obstruction by fear, 71–72, 72–73, 78
  as purpose of freedom, 129–130
Perception
  conditioning of, 86
  making changes in, 96–98, 109
  management of, 81–82
  stress as product of, 80–81
Permian Era, 147
Pharaohs, 7
Photosynthesis, 6, 7, 22, 33, 126, 137

Photo Credits

About the Author

Peter Russell gained a first-class honors degree in theoretical physics and psychology at the University of Cambridge, England, where he studied for a time with Stephen Hawking. He then earned a master's degree in computer science, also from the University of Cambridge. Russell subsequently studied meditation and Eastern philosophy in India, and on his return to England, conducted research into the neurophysiology of meditation at the University of Bristol.

As an author and lecturer, Peter Russell has explored the potentials of human consciousness—always integrating Eastern wisdom with the facts of Western science—and sharing with audiences worldwide his innovative discoveries and insights about the nature of consciousness, personal transformation, global change, and human evolution.

Russell was also one of the first to present self-development programs in business. Over the past ten years, he has been a consultant to IBM, Apple Computer, Shell, British Petroleum, Barclays Bank, American Express, British Telecom, Volvo, and other major international corporations.

Peter Russell's previous works include *The TM Technique, The Brain Book, The Upanishads, The Global Brain, The Creative Manager, The White Hole in Time*, and *From Science to God*. His books are used as required reading at a number of universities, and are translated into numerous languages. As a futurist, he has been a keynote speaker at many international conferences in Europe and the U.S. He has also created award-winning videos based on *The Global Brain* and *The White Hole in Time*.

Give the Gift of *Waking Up in Time* to Your Friends

ORDER FORM

❑ Yes, I want _____ copies of *Waking Up in Time* at $17.95 each
plus $3.50 shipping for the first book and $1.00 for each
additional book. California residents add 8¼% sales tax.

Name _____

Company _____

Address _____

City _____ State _____ Zip _____

Phone _____

Total $ _____

❑ Check or money order enclosed

Please charge my   ❑ Visa   ❑ MasterCard

Card # _____ Exp. _____

Signature _____

Call our Toll Free order line: 1-888-267-4446
Order online: www.originpress.com

Please make your check payable and return to:
Origin Press
PO Box 151117
San Rafael, CA 94915